# WORLDLY WORDS

## AN ANTHOLOGY OF
## AMERICAN NATURE WRITING

edited by
### Scott Slovic

Fumikura Press

# Acknowledgments

In 1993, the Macmillan Publishing Company produced an anthology called *Being in the World: An Environmental Reader for Writers* that I edited with Professor Terrell Dixon from the University of Houston. Often, during my stay in Japan from September 1993 until August 1994, people asked me if *Being in the World* might be an appropriate textbook for Japanese students, a way of introducing them not only to American written English but to contemporary thoughts about the natural world. Although many of the essays in *Being in the World* seemed potentially interesting to Japanese students, the anthology itself —at 726 pages—is much too big for an average English class. (Even American classes tend to pick and choose specific selections from the book rather than using the entire collection.) Upon hearing the tremendous size of *Being in the World*, Japanese scholars often said to me, "That's much too big for our purposes. Why don't you make a new, smaller anthology that we can use to introduce our students to American nature writing?" *Worldly Words: An Anthology of American Nature Writing* is the book that resulted from this suggestion. I am very grateful to Fumikura Press for undertaking this project, especially to Professors Joji Okanda, Kunio Nakamura, and Masataka Ota, who have been my main contacts with the press.

The Japanese branch of the Association for the Study of Literature and Environment (ASLE-J) was established in May 1994, and I wish I had space here to acknowledge the many, many scholars—ASLE-J members and not—who supported me during my stay in Japan and led me to believe that making this anthology for Japanese students would be a worthwhile project. Let me at least mention a handful of people who have been particularly helpful. My visit to Japan might never have happened had it not been for the generous hospitality of Professor Toshio Watanabe from the University of Tokyo, Professors Ken Akiyama and Kazu Nagamori from Sophia University, and Professor Shoji Goto from Rikkyo University. At each of these universities, I had wonderful colleagues such as Takaki Hiraishi ("Todai") and Shinji Watanabe (Rikkyo) whose support enabled me to "spread the word" about American nature writing to many students at these universities. I spent much of my time in Japan travelling around the country, lecturing on nature writing to students, scholars, and the general public. Some people were especially helpful in inviting me to give special lectures. I would like, in particular, to thank Professors Masatoshi Miyashita, Takashi Tsuchinaga, and Akira Ito (Hokkaido University), Professor Naoki Ishihata (Tohoku University), Professor Tsutomu Iwata (Koka Women's College), Professor Katsunori Yamazato (University of the Ryukyus), Professor Katsumi Kamioka (Kochi University), Professor Hisashi Noda (Kyushu Institute of Technology), Professor Bernd Stevens Richter (Miyazaki International College), Professor Takashi Kinoshita (Ehime University), Professor Minoru Iida (Shinshu University), Professor Ken-ichi Takada (Aoyama Gakuin University), Professor Masahiko Narita (Senshu University), and Professor Kay Hetherly (Showa Women's University). In her role as president of the Thoreau Society of Japan, Professor Akiko Tokuza from Tokyo Keizai University has helped to support the study of nature writing in general, and I appreciate her kindness and openmindedness. Professors John Robbins and (my uncle) Harold G. Slovic, both from Aichi Gakusen University, have also been very helpful as I've worked to bring American nature writing to the Japanese islands. Members of the Tokyo Nature Writing Study Group— including Professors Michiyo Ishii, Naomi Tonooka, Saeko Ikemoto, Masahiko Narita, and Bruce Allen, and my students Miho Sato, Mariko Ohmi, and Yuko Aihara—are at the center of this new scholarly interest in nature writing. Professors Kiyotoshi Murakami (Kanazawa University); Takayuki Tatsumi and Midori Asahina (Keio University); and Kazuto Ono, Tsutomu Takahashi, and Izumi Ogura (Kyushu University) have provided important guidance and encouragement. Mr. Shigeyuki Okajima and Mr. Nobuhiro Sato have supported the study of American nature writing from their positions outside of academia. I wish I could name all of the friends and colleagues who, directly or indirectly, contributed to the existence of *Worldly Words,* and I hope those whom I do not have space to mention will realize that I do appreciate their help.

I am grateful to Professors Katsumi Kamioka, Shogo Ikuta, Joji Okanda, and Yuri Yokota for their help in annotating the selections in this anthology—their work is crucial to the usefulness of this collection. In July 1994, a few days before my return to Texas, I presented the special neckties that I wore during my lectures in Japan (a rhapsodic lake scene drawn by a child and a Jeremiadic image of a solitary, howling wolf) to Professor Shoko Itoh from Hiroshima University and Professor Ken-ichi Noda from Kanazawa University, in the hope that these good friends and excellent scholars would "carry the torch" of American nature writing in Japan after my departure. I am pleased to see that they are doing so.

Finally, I wish to thank the Japan-United States Educational Commission for the Fulbright award that made my stay in Japan possible. My friend and mentor, Professor Barton Levi St. Armand from Brown University, has facilitated my contacts with the Fulbright Commission and the Japanese scholarly community in every possible way. And, as always, I thank my wife Analinda and my son Jacinto for their steadfast love and for tolerating my busy life as the "Johnny Appleseed of nature writing."

Scott Slovic

# CONTENTS

# Introduction

Could it be, I like to ask my students—could it be that "the most important function of literature today is to redirect human consciousness to a full consideration of its place in a threatened natural world"?

The American scholar Glen A. Love, from the University of Oregon, made this claim in an influential 1990 article called "Revaluing Nature: Toward an Ecological Criticism." The purpose of university teaching, of teaching at any level, is to ask challenging questions and to instruct students to ask important questions of themselves and the world—teaching is not the same as *preaching*. And yet it has become increasingly clear to me during my career as a professor of American literature that literature is, indeed, much more than an aesthetic toy, created for the pleasure of clever, but "irresponsible," critics and students who resist taking stances on what's happening in the world. Literary scholarship and literature itself are, on the most fundamental level, associated with human values and attitudes. Writers write in order to express a particular worldview, a set of beliefs about the way the world is or ought to be. It seems, therefore, that teachers and students of literature should consider how literary expression provokes and guides readers to decide what is important and meaningful to them.

That's what I spent 1993-94 doing when I taught American environmental literature as a Fulbright visiting professor at the University of Tokyo, Rikkyo University, Sophia University, and Kanazawa University. And the following anthology is intended to give teachers and students in Japan a tool for continuing this exploration. I have selected twelve essays for this collection that will introduce readers to both prominent recent nature writers (such as Edward Abbey, Annie Dillard, Wendell Berry, Barry Lopez, Terry Tempest Williams, and John Elder) and up-and-coming writers who deserve to have a larger audience (for instance, Betsy Hilbert, David Roberts, and Martin W. Lewis). I have made a point of including important Native American (Linda Hogan and Marilou Awiakta) and Mexican American (Ray Gonzalez) nature writers in order to demonstrate that different cultural groups within the United States have their own distinctive perspectives on the natural world.

In April 1994, just before Earth Day, I read the following comment by Mikhail Gorbachev, the former president of the Soviet Union who is now president of the environmental organization called Green Cross International: "The process of self-destruction of the foundations of human development has gone too far. ... We need a new system of values." A new system of values. What should such a system consist of and where can we find it? I would argue that nature writing (that is, literary nonfiction—essays—about the relationship between human beings and the nonhuman, natural world), literature in general, and other environmentally-conscious artforms (folksongs, landscape painting, even some kinds of sculpture) are essential to the process of developing a new system of values, one that will help us to achieve what ecologists call a "sustainable society."

When Glen Love argued that "the most important function of literature today is to redirect human consciousness to a full consideration of its place in a threatened natural world," he did not limit his claim to *American* literature, but implied that writers in every country—as well as artists and scholars working in other media and disciplines —must assume responsibility for guiding their audiences to a deeper, more disciplined relationship with nonhuman nature. Many writers resist the political dimension of their subject matter—their primary goal is "art," not "diatribe." Sometimes, though, the very best writers decide there's a time for art and another time for politics, for taking a stand to defend something that's important and in danger—like a forest scheduled for clearcutting or an endangered species. Rick Bass, a leading young fiction writer and essayist from the state of Montana, made this comment in 1993: "Suppose you are given a bucket of water. You're standing

there holding it. Your home's on fire. Will you pour the
cool water over the flames or will you sit there and write a
poem about it?" For nature writers, the "bucket of water"
in this scenario stands for their language, their writing; and
the "home" Bass is talking about is both the specific place
where the individual writer lives and the planet as a whole.
Although most of the top-notch contemporary nature writers are interested in fundamental epistemological questions, in understanding the place of human individuals and
human societies in the larger cosmos, many of these writers
have become increasingly political as they recognize potential (and actual) environmental catastrophes in the here-
and-now. The general structure of this book moves from
essays on how we experience nature (epistemological
nature writing) to pieces that explore more explicitly how
human behavior protects or damages the nonhuman environment (political nature writing).

Nature writing is a literary genre with a long history in
North America—the oral tales of Native Americans and
even the earliest written documents of Europeans arriving
in the "New World" (diaries, letters, official reports, and
sermons) were often a form of nature writing, exploring the
relationships between people and animals and landscapes.
Henry David Thoreau, who lived from 1817 to 1862 in
Concord, Massachusetts, is generally singled out as the
most important literary ancestor of contemporary

American nature writers. In such classic works as *Walden* (1854) and *The Maine Woods* (1864), Thoreau anticipated many of the central ideas and issues that are routinely observed in American nature writing of the past fifty years: for instance, concern about the effect of industry and technology on the natural world and human society; fascination with the relationship between the human mind and nonhuman nature; emphasis on local, everyday phenomena rather than exotic, extraordinary things and events; and appreciation of simplicity in nature and human life. In the past quarter-century, beginning with Edward Abbey's *Desert Solitaire: A Season in the Wilderness* (1968), there has been a veritable "renaissance" of important environmental writing in the United States—poetry, fiction, and especially literary nonfiction (essays). Major essayists working in this field today include Barry Lopez, Wendell Berry, Annie Dillard, Peter Matthiessen, Ann Zwinger, Gary Snyder, Scott Russell Sanders, Robert Finch, David Quammen, John Hay, N. Scott Momaday, William Kittredge, David Rains Wallace, Robert Michael Pyle, Leslie Marmon Silko, John Daniel, Terry Tempest Williams, Gary Nabhan, and Linda Hogan, to name only a few. Several Japanese publishing companies have been actively preparing translations of American nature writing in recent years, and in the coming year translations of such important books as Edward Abbey's *The Journey Home: Some Words in Defense of the*

*American West* (1977), Terry Tempest Williams's *Refuge: An Unnatural History of Family and Place* (1991), and Robert Finch's *Common Ground* (1981) will appear. A few years ago, John A. Murray, a scholar from the University of Alaska, wrote that "Since the first Earth Day on April 22, 1970, a once obscure prose genre—nature writing—has steadily grown in stature and popularity until, in 1992, it is arguably *the* major genre in American literature." Many scholars would agree with Murray's bold claim.

I often wonder what should be the appropriate response to environmental literature (that is, poetry, fiction, and drama as well as essays) in America and in other countries like Japan. As I mentioned above, one of the tendencies that contemporary nature writers have inherited from Henry David Thoreau is the concern for the local and familiar, not just the distant and exotic. For some, like the Kentucky writer Wendell Berry, this idea is essential; "the question that must be addressed," he wrote in 1989, "is not how to care for the planet but how to care for each of the planet's millions of human and natural neighborhoods, each of its millions of small pieces and parcels of land, each one of which is in some precious way different from all the others." The ability to evoke the subtle mysteries of specific "neighborhoods" is one of the great contributions of nature writing to American culture. Scientists have long realized that environmental problems are *global* problems, that loss of biodiversity, rainforest destruction, pollution, global warming, overpopulation, and other problems are of such magnitude that they have little to do with national borders. But we, as individuals and communities, can best respond to global environmental degradation by developing a strong, respectful "sense of place" in our own particular part of the world, whether that might be Berry's Kentucky farm, the hill country of central Texas where I live, the sprawling suburbs of Greater Tokyo, or the mountain villages of Nagano Prefecture. We must begin by noticing and caring for our own neighborhoods. Nature writing helps us to do so.

That's why I spent a year teaching American nature writing in Japan—not simply to be a kind of travel agent, encouraging Japanese students to read *Desert Solitaire* and then visit Abbey's Utah or to read Norman Maclean's *A River Runs Through It* and then seize the next opportunity to see the rivers of Montana. American nature writing can help people appreciate wild things, wild places, no matter where the readers happen to live, just as Japanese nature writing can contribute to readers' awareness and appreciation of nature all over the world. What is Japanese nature writing? This is one of the main questions that the Japanese branch of the Association for the Study of Literature and Environment (ASLE-Japan), founded in May 1994, is currently asking. I would encourage readers interested in

Japanese nature writing to begin looking for literature on such subjects as fishing, hunting, farming, gardening/gardens, insects and animals (including specific activities like bird-watching), rocks, traveling, boating, mountain climbing, walking, weather/seasons, and even responses to technology and urban surroundings. There should be a wealth of this.

I spent 1993-94 in one of the world's most intensely urban environments, occasionally sneaking away to cross-country ski in Hokkaido and Tohoku, to wade in the pale blue waters of Okinawa and southeastern Kyushu, and to crawl through dripping caves such as Ryūgado in Shikoku and in Akikawa Keikoku, not far from Tokyo. But I always had to return to the megacity for discussions of "nature" (a quaint, distant abstraction) in the windowless, smoky bars of Shinjuku. At the end of June, two nature writing scholars from Shikoku arranged for me to visit eighty-four-year-old farmer and writer Masanobu Fukuoka, the author of *The One-Straw Revolution*, in the mountains outside of Matsuyama. After spending a few hours walking around the jungle-like orchards with Fukuoka-san, we went to have tea in a primitive hut. While drinking tea, we listened to Fukuoka-san talk about farming and nature. Then I asked him something I had been wondering during our entire visit to his mountain place. Did he think it might be possible for the university to contribute anything to our under-

standing of nature? (What did he think about these three literature professors who had come to visit him?) Fukuoka-
san seemed to look right past me, and then he said, "Listen
to the bird sing." I thought he simply hadn't heard my
question or that he found it unimportant. But everyone
stopped talking and, sure enough, there was a nightingale
calling outside the hut. Then Fukuoka-san's assistant
leaned over to me and whispered, "He means, it is possible
if you have a simple mind." In other words, those of us who
work at universities might be able to contribute to society's
understanding of nature if we remember to pay attention to
nature itself, if we don't lose ourselves in words, theories,
texts, laboratories. A powerful admonition.

Some of my friends—fellow nature writing scholars—
think the human species is destined to destroy itself, perhaps even to make the earth uninhabitable. I tend to be
guardedly optimistic, though—and that's because I hope
we have the wisdom to heed our environmental literature
and allow it to guide us in redesigning human communities
with an eye to the distant future, communities whose principal aim is to avoid exhausting and despoiling planetary
resources. But we must remember to do more than read.
We must also "listen to the bird sing."

## About the Editor

Born in 1960, Scott Slovic grew up in Eugene, Oregon. He studied at Stanford University, was a Fulbright Research Scholar at the University of Bonn (Germany), and earned his M.A. and Ph.D. in American literature at Brown University. He has been an associate professor of English at Southwest Texas State University in San Marcos, just south of Austin. His many publications include *Seeking Awareness in American Nature Writing: Henry Thoreau, Annie Dillard, Edward Abbey, Wendell Berry, Barry Lopez* (University of Utah Press, 1992) and *Being in the World: An Environmental Reader for Writers* (Macmillan, 1993). Since October 1992, Slovic has served as the founding president of the Association for the Study of Literature and Environment (ASLE), a scholarly society that now has more than 600 members from around the world. He helped to organize a Japanese branch of ASLE in May 1994, while he was teaching at the University of Tokyo, Sophia University, Rikkyo University, and Kanazawa University as a Visiting Fulbright Senior Lecturer. He is taking a new teaching position at the University of Nevada-Reno in the fall of 1995.

# Living Like Weasels
(1982)

## Annie Dillard

꙰

A weasel is wild. Who knows what he thinks? He sleeps in his underground den, his tail draped over his nose. Sometimes he lives in his den for two days without leaving. Outside, he stalks rabbits, mice, muskrats, and birds, killing more bodies than he can eat warm, and often dragging the carcasses home. Obedient to instinct, he bites his prey at the neck, either splitting the jugular vein at the throat or crunching the brain at the base of the skull, and he does not let go. One naturalist refused to kill a weasel who was socketed into his hand deeply as a rattlesnake. The man could in no way pry the tiny weasel off, and he had to walk half a mile to water, the weasel dangling from his palm, and soak him off like a stubborn label.

And once, says Ernest Thompson Seton—once, a man shot an eagle out of the sky. He examined the eagle and found the dry skull of a weasel fixed by the jaws to his throat. The supposition is that the eagle had pounced on the weasel and the weasel swiveled and bit as instinct taught him, tooth to neck, and nearly won. I would like to have seen that eagle from the air a few weeks or months before he was shot: was the whole weasel still attached to his feathered throat, a fur pendant? Or did the eagle eat what he could reach, gutting the living weasel with his talons before his breast, bending his beak, cleaning the beautiful airborne bones?

I have been reading about weasels because I saw one last week. I startled a weasel who startled me, and we exchanged a long glance.

Twenty minutes from my house, through the woods by the quarry and across the highway, is Hollins Pond, a remarkable piece of shallowness, where I like to go at sunset and sit on a tree trunk. Hollins Pond is also called Murray's Pond; it covers two acres of bottomland near Tinker Creek with six inches of water and six thousand lily pads. In winter, brown-and-white steers stand in the middle of it, merely dampening their hooves; from the distant shore they look like miracle itself, complete with miracle's nonchalance. Now, in summer, the steers are gone. The water lilies have blossomed and spread to a green horizontal plane that is terra firma to plodding blackbirds, and tremulous ceiling to black leeches, crayfish, and carp.

This is, mind you, suburbia. It is a five-minute walk in three directions to rows of houses, though none is visible here. There's a 55 mph highway at one end of the pond, and a nesting pair of wood ducks at the other. Under every bush is a muskrat hole or a beer can. The far end is an alternating series of fields and woods, fields and woods, threaded everywhere with motorcycle tracks—in whose bare clay wild turtles lay eggs.

So. I had crossed the highway, stepped over two low barbed-wire fences, and traced the motorcycle path in all gratitude through the wild rose and poison ivy of the pond's shoreline up into high grassy fields. Then I cut down through the woods to the mossy fallen tree where I sit. This tree is excellent. It makes a dry, upholstered bench at the upper, marshy end of the pond, a plush jetty raised from the thorny shore between a shallow blue body of water and a deep blue body of sky.

The sun had just set. I was relaxed on the tree trunk, ensconced in the lap of lichen, watching the lily pads at my feet tremble and part dreamily over the thrusting path of a carp. A yellow bird appeared to my right and flew behind me. It caught my eye; I swiveled around—and the next instant, inexplicably, I was looking down at a weasel, who was looking up at me.

Weasel! I'd never seen one wild before. He was ten inches long, thin as a curve, a muscled ribbon, brown as fruitwood, soft-furred, alert. His face was fierce, small and pointed as a lizard's; he would have made a good arrowhead. There was just a dot of chin, maybe two brown hairs' worth, and then the pure white fur began that spread down his underside. He had two black eyes I didn't see, any more than you see a window.

The weasel was stunned into stillness as he was emerging from beneath an enormous shaggy wild rose bush four feet away. I was stunned into stillness twisted backward on the tree trunk. Our eyes locked, and someone threw away the key.

Our look was as if two lovers, or deadly enemies, met unexpectedly on an overgrown path when each had been thinking of something else: a clearing blow to the gut. It was also a bright blow to the brain, or a sudden beating of brains, with all the charge and intimate grate of rubbed balloons. It emptied our lungs. It felled the forest, moved the fields, and drained the pond; the world dismantled and tumbled into that black hole of eyes. If you and I looked at each other that way, our skulls would split and drop to our shoulders. But we don't. We keep our skulls. So.

He disappeared. This was only last week, and already I don't remember what shattered the enchantment. I think I blinked, I think I retrieved my brain from the weasel's brain, and tried to memorize what I was seeing, and the weasel felt the yank of separation, the careening splashdown into real life and the urgent current of instinct. He vanished under the wild rose. I waited motionless, my mind suddenly full of data and my spirit with pleadings, but he didn't return.

Please do not tell me about "approach-avoidance conflicts." I tell you I've been in that weasel's brain for sixty seconds, and he was in mine. Brains are private places, muttering through unique and secret tapes—but the weasel and I both plugged into another tape simultaneously, for a sweet and shocking time. Can I help it if it was a blank?

What goes on in his brain the rest of the time? What does a weasel think about? He won't say. His journal is tracks in clay, a spray of feathers, mouse blood and bone: uncollected, unconnected, loose-leaf, and blown.

I would like to learn, or remember, how to live. I come to Hollins Pond not so much to learn how to live as, frankly, to forget about it. That is, I don't think I can learn from a wild animal how to live in particular—shall I suck warm blood, hold my tail high, walk with my footprints precisely over the prints of my hands? —but I might learn something of mindlessness, something of the purity of living in the physical senses and the dignity of living without bias or motive. The weasel lives in necessity and we live in choice, hating necessity and dying at the last ignobly in its talons. I would like to live as I should, as the weasel lives as he should. And I suspect that for me the way is like the weasel's: open to time and death painlessly, noticing everything, remembering nothing, choosing the given with a fierce and pointed will.

I missed my chance. I should have gone for the throat. I should have lunged for that streak of white under the weasel's chin and held on, held on through mud and into the wild rose, held on for a dearer life. We could live under the wild rose wild as weasels, mute and uncomprehending. I could very calmly go wild. I could live two days in the den, curled, leaning on mouse fur, sniffing bird bones, blinking, licking, breathing musk, my hair tangled in the roots of grasses. Down is a good place to go, where the mind is single. Down is out, out of your ever-loving mind and back to your careless senses. I remember muteness as a prolonged and giddy fast, where every moment is a feast of utterance received. Time and events are merely poured, unremarked, and ingested directly, like blood pulsed into my gut through a jugular vein. Could two live that way? Could two live under the wild rose, and explore by the pond, so that the smooth mind of each is as everywhere present to the other, and as received and as unchallenged, as falling snow?

We could, you know. We can live any way we want. People take vows of poverty, chastity, and obedience—even of silence—by choice. The thing is to stalk your calling in a certain skilled and supple way, to locate the most tender and live spot and plug into that pulse. This is yielding, not fighting. A weasel doesn't "attack" anything; a weasel lives as he's meant to, yielding at every moment to the perfect freedom of single necessity.

I think it would be well, and proper, and obedient, and pure, to grasp your one necessity and not let it go, to dangle from it limp wherever it takes you. Then even death, where you're going no matter how you live, cannot you part. Seize it and let it seize you up aloft even, till your eyes burn out and drop; let your musky flesh fall off in shreds, and let your very bones unhinge and scatter, loosened over fields, over fields and woods, lightly, thoughtless, from any height at all, from as high as eagles.

## Topics for Discussion and Writing

1. In the second section of the essay ("I have been reading..."), Dillard mentions that her encounter with the weasel happened in "suburbia." Discuss in class the significance of an encounter with "wildness" in an area so close to a city, or write a short essay on the importance of the suburban location.

2. Have you ever met a "wild creature" in either a city or out in a rural place? Write a narrative in which you tell the story of this experience. If you have never had such an encounter, go out and look for an animal—if not a weasel or a bear, then perhaps a butterfly or a crow—and then write about it. Explain why it's meaningful to make contact with animals that have lives independent of human control. Is this possible even in big cities?

3. Look at the conclusion of Dillard's essay and examine closely the meaning she derives from her experience with the weasel. Is this essay a scientific analysis of weasels or a reflection on the symbolic meaning of this animal for an imaginative human observer? Discuss Dillard's final message in class. Is it somehow relevant to your own life?

4. Often we discover amazing things while we are in the middle of our everyday activities. Write a paper in which you recall an ordinary experience—riding the subway, having a meal with your family, walking in a garden—that led you to make an important realization about the world.

# Apologia

(1992)

## Barry Lopez

ॐ

A few miles east of home in the Cascades I slow down and pull over for two raccoons, sprawled still on stones in the road. I carry them to the side and lay them in sun-shot, windblown grass in the barrow pit. In eastern Oregon, along U.S. 20, black-tailed jackrabbits lie like welts of sod—three, four, then a fifth. By the bridge over Jordan Creek, just shy of the Idaho border, in the drainage of the Owyhee River, a crumpled adolescent porcupine leers up almost maniacally over its blood-flecked teeth. I carry each one away from the tarmac into a cover of grass or brush out of decency, I think. And worry. Who are these animals, their lights gone out? What journeys have fallen apart here?

I do not stop to remove each dark blister from the road. I wince before the recently dead, feel my lips tighten, see something else, a fence post, in the spontaneous aversion of my eyes, and pull over. I imagine white silk threads of life still vibrating inside them, even if the body's husk is stretched out for yards, stuck like oiled muslin to the road. The energy that held them erect leaves like a bullet; but the memory of that energy fades slowly from the wrinkled cornea, the bloodless fur.

The raccoons and, later, a red fox carry like sacks of wet gravel and sand. Each animal is like a solitary child's shoe in the road.

Once a man asked, Why do you bother? You never know, I said. The ones you give some semblance of burial, to whom you offer an apology, may have been like seers in a parallel culture. It is an act of respect, a technique of awareness.

In Idaho I hit a young sage sparrow—*thwack* against the right fender in the very split second I see it. Its companion rises a foot higher from the same spot, slow as smoke, and sails off clean into the desert. I rest the walloped bird in my left hand, my right thumb pressed to its chest. I feel for the wail of the heart. Its eyes glisten like rain on crystal. Nothing but warmth. I shut the tiny eyelids and lay it beside a clump of bunchgrass. Beyond a barbed-wire fence the overgrazed range is littered with cow flops. The road curves away to the south. I nod before I go, a ridiculous gesture, out of simple grief.

I pass four spotted skunks. The swirling air is acrid

with the rupture of each life.

Darkness rises in the valleys of Idaho. East of Grand View, south of the Snake River, nighthawks swoop the road for gnats, silent on the wing as owls. On a descending curve I see two of them lying soft as clouds in the road. I turn around and come back. The sudden slowing down and my K-turn at the bottom of the hill draw the attention of a man who steps away from a tractor, a dozen yards from where the birds lie. I can tell by his step, the suspicious tilt of his head, that he is wary, vaguely proprietary. Offended, or irritated, he may throw the birds back into the road when I leave. So I wait, subdued like a penitent, a body in each hand.

He speaks first, a low voice, a deep murmur weighted with awe. He has been watching these flocks feeding just above the road for several evenings. He calls them whip-poorwills. He gestures for a carcass. How odd, yes, the way they concentrate their hunting right on the road, I say. He runs a finger down the smooth arc of the belly and remarks on the small whiskered bill. He pulls one long wing out straight, but not roughly. He marvels. He glances at my car, baffled by this out-of-state courtesy. Two dozen night-hawks career past, back and forth at arm's length, feeding at our height and lower. He asks if I would mind—as though I owned it—if he took the bird up to the house to show his wife. "She's never seen anything like this." He's fascinated. "Not close."

I trust, later, he will put it in the fields, not throw the body in the trash, a whirligig.

North of Pinedale in western Wyoming on U.S. 189, below the Gros Ventre Range, I see a big doe from a great distance, the low rays of first light gleaming in her tawny reddish hair. She rests askew, like a crushed tree. I drag her to the shoulder, then down a long slope by the petals of her ears. A gunnysack of plaster mud, ears cold as rain gutters. All of her doesn't come. I climb back up for the missing leg. The stain of her is darker than the black asphalt. The stains go north and off to the south as far as I can see.

On an afternoon trafficless, quiet as a cloister, headed across South Pass in the Wind River Range, I swerve violently but hit an animal, and then try to wrestle the gravel-spewing skid in a straight line along the lip of an embankment. I know even as I struggle for control the irony of this: I could pitch off here to my own death, easily. The bird is dead somewhere in the road behind me. Only a few seconds and I am safely back on the road, nauseated, light-headed.

It is hard to distinguish among younger gulls. I turn this one around slowly in my hands. It could be a Western gull, a mew gull, a California gull. I do not remember well enough the bill markings, the color of the legs. I have no doubt about the vertebrae shattered beneath the seamless white of its ropy neck.

East of Lusk, Wyoming, in Nebraska, I stop for a badger. I squat on the macadam to admire the long claws, the perfect set of its teeth in the broken jaw, the ramulose shading of its fur—how it differs slightly, as does every badger's, from the drawings and pictures in the field guides. A car drifts toward us over the prairie, coming on in the other lane, a white 1962 Chevrolet station wagon. The driver slows to pass. In the bright sunlight I can't see his face, only an arm and the gesture of his thick left hand. It opens in a kind of shrug, hangs briefly in limp sadness, then extends itself in supplication. Gone past, it curls into itself against the car door and is still.

Farther on in western Nebraska I pick up the small bodies of mice and birds. While I wait to retrieve these creatures I do not meet the eyes of passing drivers. Whoever they are, I feel anger toward them, in spite of the sparrow and the gull I myself have killed. We treat the attrition of lives on the road like the attrition of lives in war: horrifying, unavoidable, justified. Accepting the slaughter leaves people momentarily fractious, embarrassed. South of Broken Bow, at dawn, I cannot avoid an immature barn swallow. It hangs by its head, motionless in the slats of the grill.

I stop for a rabbit on Nebraska 806 and find, only a few

feet away, a garter snake. What else have I missed, too small, too narrow? What has gone under or past me while I stared at mountains, hay meadows, fencerows, the beryl surface of rivers? In Wyoming I could not help but see pronghorn antelope swollen big as barrels by the side of the road, their legs splayed rigidly aloft. For animals that large people will stop. But how many have this habit of clearing the road of smaller creatures, people who would remove the ones I miss? I do not imagine I am alone. As much sorrow as the man's hand conveyed in Nebraska, it meant gratitude too for burying the dead.

Still, I do not wish to meet anyone's eyes.


In southwestern Iowa, outside Clarinda, I haul a deer into high grass out of sight of the road and begin to examine it. It is still whole, but the destruction is breathtaking. The skull, I soon discover, is fractured in four places; the jaw, hanging by shreds of mandibular muscle, is broken at the symphysis, beneath the incisors. The pelvis is crushed, the left hind leg unsocketed. All but two ribs are dislocated along the vertebral column, which is complexly fractured. The intestines have been driven forward into the chest. The heart and lungs have ruptured the chest wall at the base of the neck. The signature of a tractor-trailer truck: 78,000 pounds at 65 mph.

In front of a motel room in Ottumwa I finger-scrape

the dry stiff carcasses of bumblebees, wasps, and butterflies from the grill and headlight mountings, and I scrub with a wet cloth to soften and wipe away the nap of crumbles, the insects, the aerial plankton of spiders and mites. I am uneasy carrying so many of the dead. The carnage is so obvious.

In Illinois, west of Kankakee, two raccoons as young as the ones in Oregon. In Indiana another raccoon, a gray squirrel. When I make the left turn into the driveway at the house of a friend outside South Bend, it is evening, hot and muggy. I can hear cicadas in a lone elm. I'm glad to be here.

From the driveway entrance I look back down Indiana 23, toward Indiana 8, remembering the farm roads of Illinois and Iowa. I remember how beautiful it was in the limpid air to drive Nebraska 2 through the Sand Hills, to see how far at dusk the land was etched east and west of Wyoming 28. I remember the imposition of the Wind River Range in a hard, blue sky beneath white ranks of buttonhook clouds, windy hay fields on the Snake River Plain, the welcome of Russian olive trees and willows in creek bottoms. The transformation of the heart such beauty engenders is not enough tonight to let me shed the heavier memory, a catalog too morbid to write out, too vivid to ignore.

I stand in the driveway now, listening to the cicadas whirring in the dark tree. My hands grip the sill of the open window at the driver's side, and I lean down as if to speak to someone still sitting there. The weight I wish to fall I cannot fathom, a sorrow over the world's dark hunger.

A light comes on over the porch. I hear a dead bolt thrown, the shiver of a door pulled free. The words of atonement I pronounce are too inept to offer me release. Or forgiveness. My friend is floating across the tree-shadowed lawn. What is to be done with the desire for exculpation?

"Later than we thought you'd be," he says.

I do not want the lavabo. I wish to make amends.

"I made more stops than I thought I would," I answer.

"Well, bring this in. And whatever I can take," he says.

I anticipate, in the powerful antidote of our conversation, the reassurance of a human enterprise, the forgiving embrace of the rational. It waits within, beyond the slow tail-wagging of two dogs standing at the screen door.

## Topics for Discussion and Writing

1. When asked why he stops to bury animals that he finds dead on country roads, Lopez replies, "The ones you give some semblance of burial, to whom you offer an apology, may have been like seers in a parallel culture. It is an act of respect, a technique of awareness." Discuss this idea in class. How can such acts of "awareness" transform modern human civilization? How can they change the daily experience of individual people?

2. In the second section of his essay, Lopez recounts the experience of finding two dead nighthawks while driving through Idaho farm country. A farmer (driving a tractor) approaches the author suspiciously, but when he looks closely at the dead birds, he feels a sense of fascination, even awe. Explain the significance of this scene. How does it illustrate the goal of Lopez's writing?

3. At the end of his essay, Lopez suggests that he feels not only a great burden of responsibility for the animals that he and other drivers kill on the road, but a "desire for exculpation" (a wish to be relieved of guilt). The narrator's perspective in this essay is one of extreme morality, extreme respect and awareness—like that of a monk. What would society be like if all of us acted/thought in this way?

4. Take a moment while you are out walking, bicycling, or driving to stop and notice a dead animal along the road or sidewalk. Or pause at home to examine and think about a dead insect you happen to find. Conduct a Lopez-like burial (or imagine yourself doing this), and write a paper describing and explaining this activity.

# Five Days on Mount Huntington
## (1967)

## David Roberts

ঞ

On July 29, 1965, it dawned perfectly clear again, the fifth such day in a row. In the small tent pitched on a three foot ledge of ice beneath the huge granite overhang, Don Jensen and Ed Bernd prepared for an early start. They were tired from the strenuous pace of the last few days, but with the weather holding so remarkably, they knew they shouldn't waste an hour. By 7:30A.M. they had begun climbing up the line of stirrups fixed on the overhang, the crux of the whole west face, which Matt Hale had skillfully led three days before. They were short on pitons and fixed ropes, but they were carrying the bivouac tent, in hopes of a chance to reach the summit of Mount Huntington. They knew that Matt and I would be bringing up equipment from our lower camp that day, but they couldn't afford to wait for it.

It took only a short while for both of them to top the

overhang; but as soon as they had, Ed realized he'd forgotten his ice axe. A moment's pause—then they decided to go on without it. They alternated pitches, the leader using Don's axe, the second only a long ice piton. They were on a sixty-degree ice slope, patched with small rock outcroppings. They climbed well, chopping small steps, using only a belay piton at the top of each pitch. On the second, Don could place nothing better than a short soft-iron knife-blade, which he had to tie off. They left fixed ropes on the first three pitches, then saved their last one for the final cliff. Almost before they expected it, they were at the foot of it. Don took the lead. As Ed belayed, facing out, he could survey the throng of unnamed peaks to the south, and look almost straight down to the floor of the Tokositna Glacier, 5000 feet below his feet. Don started up the pitch boldly, swinging on his hands around a corner of the rough, solid granite, and placed a good piton. He used only two more above that, both for aid: the first, a shaky stirrup on a blank spot; the second, a hundred feet above Ed, a tiny knife-blade as a handhold by which he pulled himself up to the top of the cliff. Ed knew it was a magnificent lead, and he must have thrilled at Don's competence. In his turn he led up a steep snow fluting, and suddenly emerged on the bare, sweeping summit icefield. It rose, completely smooth, at a fifty-degree angle toward the mountain's summit. Quickly they climbed four pitches, but the ice was already starting to melt in the early afternoon sun. They stopped at the only rock outcrop in the whole expanse, and pitched the bivouac tent on a tiny ledge. There they sat, cooking a pot of soup on their laps, as the sun slanted toward the western horizon, toward Mounts Hunter and Foraker. As accustomed as they were by now to that sight, it must have seemed almost new this time, with the summit in reach for the first time in a month. After sunset they would start out for it, as soon as the snow had begun to freeze again.

Meanwhile, Matt and I had reached the high tent with supplies. We decided to go on above. Even if we couldn't catch up with Don and Ed, we thought we might safeguard the route for their descent. Matt noticed Ed's axe outside the tent. For a moment we were disturbed; then we decided he had simply forgotten it, so we packed it up to take with us.

Above the big overhang, we could follow the fixed ropes and the steps chopped in the ice. When I reached the top of the second pitch, I could see the anchor piton was poor. I tried to get a new one in, but there were no cracks. At last I clipped in to the eye of the bad piton—a mistake, for the fixed ropes were tied to the hero loop, not to the piton—and belayed Matt up. Matt led on. A few feet above me, he stopped to adjust his crampon. Suddenly he slipped, falling on top of me. Not very alarmed, I put up a hand to ward off his crampons and take the impact. I felt the snow ledge I was standing on break under my feet; then, abruptly, we were both falling. I was still holding Matt on belay; vaguely I realized the piton had probably pulled, but I couldn't understand why the fixed ropes weren't holding us. We gathered speed and began to bounce. Somehow I thought I was being hurt, without pain; and somehow, without fear, I anticipated the fatal plunge. But suddenly we stopped. Matt was still on top of me. Shakily we got to our feet. Now the fear came in little waves of panic. I said, almost hysterically, "We've got to get in a piton." We were standing on little knobs of rock in the middle of the clean, steep slope. Quickly I hammered in three or four pitons, none of them any good, and clipped us in. We were bruised, but not seriously hurt. However, Matt had lost one crampon and both his mittens. One of my crampons had been knocked off, but dangled from my ankle. My glasses had caught on the toe of my boot. Matt thought he had lost his axe, too, but we looked up and saw it planted in the ice where he had stopped to fix the crampon. We also saw the fixed ropes, still intact, even though the piton dangled near my feet. Then what had stopped our fall? Simultaneously we saw, almost unbelieving, that the climbing rope, dragging behind us, had snagged on one of the little knobs of rock, a rounded nubbin about the size of one's knuckle.

The discovery made us almost giddy, with a mixture of fear and astonishment at our luck. We discussed whether we should continue or descend. After a little while we decided to go on. Matt, with only one crampon, couldn't lead; but if I enlarged the right-foot steps for him, he could second. We felt very nervous as we climbed. I deliberately overprotected the route, putting in solid pitons wherever I could. We marvelled at the pitches Don and Ed had led with so few pitons, but began to worry about them a little. We climbed the last cliff as the sun, low in the sky, turned the rock golden brown. The world seemed achingly beautiful, now that we had been reprieved to see it a while longer. The hard climbing seemed to stimulate us to a breathless exhilaration, the obverse face of the panic we had just felt.

As we emerged on the summit icefield, Ed saw us from their bivouac ledge. He let out a shout. Quickly we joined them, though the slope was in dangerously bad shape, and I had to use two rock pitons in the ice for anchors. Our reunion was poignant. We kidded Ed about leaving his axe; but when we told them about our near-accident, they seemed genuinely upset. Don was confident the summit could be reached that night. For weeks we had climbed, even camped, in separate pairs, meeting only as our ropes occasionally crossed while we switched leaders. Now we might climb toward the summit together; it would be a perfect finale.

Around 10 P.M. we roped together and started up. Don led in the almost pitch-dark; I came second; Matt followed me; and Ed brought up the rear. We were inexpressibly happy to be together. This silent climb in the night to the top of the mountain seemed a superb way to share our friendship. Our excitement was contagious. We were very tired, and yet the sky was full of stars, and the air was breathlessly still. Silhouetted in the constellation Cassiopeia, Don was leading; below me, Matt and Ed competently paced their movement to fit Don's.

Shortly after midnight we reached the summit ridge. Here we could walk continuously, but only with great care, for on one hand in the eerie darkness the drop was 5000 feet, 6000 feet on the other. Don could not be sure how large the cornices were that overlooked the Ruth Glacier; not, that is, until he stuck his foot through one. He pulled it back and retreated to my ice axe belay. He was near exhaustion from a long day of leading; I took over from him.

There remained only two vertical snow cliffs, precariously carved by a year's winds. I attacked them right on the cornice, reassured by the weight of the other three belaying me. The hollow snow required brutal efforts, and took almost the last of my strength. But finally I got up them both. Then it was only three easy pitches to the summit. The light was returning; in the northeast an orange rim of flame was sweeping the tundra. As we reached the very top, the sun rose.

We were extremely tired. We sat, listless, just below the

summit, full of a dazed sense of well-being, but too tired for any celebration. Ed had brought a firecracker all the way to the top from some roadside stand in Wyoming; but we urged him not to set it off for fear it would knock the cornices loose.

It had taken us more than a month to climb Huntington's west face, a route some people had said was impossible. But people have always said things like that—our achievement had a much higher personal importance to us. It had been very difficult; the climbing had been spectacular; we had grown so discouraged that we almost abandoned the effort. But now this perfect finish, at dawn on a splendid day, together! I remember thinking even then that this was probably the best climb I could ever do, because things work out that well so rarely.

We talked to each other there, but the summit was for each of us a private experience. I do not know what Don, or Matt, or Ed felt. After an hour and a half, we started down. All the descent was anticlimactic. We wanted to hurry before the sun could melt the snow on the summit icefield. Below the bivouac tent we split again into two ropes of two. I realized how fatigued I was when I found it nearly impossible to swing out on rappel to retrieve some pitons. Finally, on the edge of exhaustion, we rappelled the overhang into our highest camp.

The four of us crowded into the two-man tent, pitched

narrow to fit on its ledge of ice. There were still thirty-five pitches below us, sixteen to our other tent. At last we could relax, but we were terribly cramped and uncomfortable. We laughed and cheered and ate all the delicacies from our food box. We even managed to sleep a bit. But the weather was deteriorating, after five perfect days. In the late afternoon Ed suggested that he and I descend to the other tent that night. I agreed.

We were off by 9: 40 P.M. A storm was evidently on its way in, and the air was relatively warm. The snow, consequently, was not in very good condition. As it grew dark, I occasionally shouted directions to Ed, who had been over these pitches only once, compared to my five times. I still felt tired, but Ed was in an exuberant mood. He said he felt he "could climb all night." We were being extra-cautious, it seemed, but this was easy going with the fixed ropes; it was even fun. We unroped to set up a rappel on the twenty-sixth pitch, a fine lead up a vertical inside corner that Don had made about two weeks before. Just before midnight on this last day of July, we chatted as Ed placed the carabiner and wound the rope around his body. We were talking about other rappels, about the first ones he had done at the Quincy Quarries back in Boston.

I said, "Just this pitch, and it's practically walking to camp."

"Yeah," he answered.

He leaned back. I heard an abrupt, jerking sound, and saw Ed's crampons spark the rock. Suddenly he was falling free below me. Without a word he fell, hit the ice fifty feet below, slid and bounced out of sight over a cliff. I shouted, but I doubt he even heard me. Suddenly he was gone. I knew he must have fallen 4000 feet, to the upper basin of the Tokositna, where no one had ever been.

I was alone. The night was empty. I shouted for Ed, but all that answered me was a mindless trickle of water near my face. I shouted for help to Don and Matt, then listened to more silence: they were too far above to hear me. I could not believe Ed was gone, and yet I could not believe anything else. I could feel the sense of shock wrapping me, like a blanket; I was seized with an urgency to do something. My first thought was to go down to look for Ed, but I put it out of my mind at once. For a moment I thought only of going up. Then it struck me that Ed was undeniably dead; therefore there was no emergency and I had to continue down.

I was without a rope, but I cut off a hank of fixed rope to tie in to the ropes below, and managed to climb down the vertical pitch. From there it was easy—but I went too fast, despite telling myself to slow down.

I reached the tent within twenty minutes after the accident. The sense of shock seemed to gather and hit me as I arrived. The tent was full of water (Matt and I had left the

back door open!). Numbly I sponged it out and got in my
sleeping bag. I took two sleeping pills. I could not figure
out what had happened. Somehow the carabiner had come
loose, for both it and the rope had disappeared with Ed. But
no piton had pulled, no jerk had come on the fixed ropes.
Out of all the mechanical explanations, all implausible, all
irrelevant to our loss, emerged only the fact that it had happened. Ed was gone.

The pills and my tiredness put me to sleep. In the
morning I woke with a dull sense of dread. The storm was
continuing, and it had begun to snow. All that day I anticipated the arrival of Matt and Don, though I knew they
would be taking their time. I became constantly nervous—
what if something had happened to them, too? The minutes
passed with agonizing slowness. I caught myself holding
my breath, listening for a sound from them. When nightfall
on August 1 came without their arrival, I was terribly dis-
appointed. Again I took sleeping pills. Again I slept in a
drugged stupor. The next day was the same; the same
white-out and lightly falling snow. I grew afraid of the
3000-foot drop beyond the door of the tent. I tied myself in
each time I had to go outside the tent. My balance seemed
poor, my hearing painfully acute. I simply waited.

Meanwhile, Don and Matt had relaxed, slept well,
eaten well. They had talked about the wonderful summit
day while they waited for the weather to break clear again.

At last, in the afternoon of August 2, they decided to pack up and descend. The pitches were in bad shape, and their heavy packs made for awkward climbing. In places the fixed ropes were coated with a solid sheath of ice.

They could see Ed's and my tracks below; and, though they could not see the tent itself, they could see that there were no tracks below it. This vaguely disturbed them, but they could think of no real cause for worry. Don noticed on the twenty-sixth pitch that some of the fixed rope had been cut off; this seemed very strange to him, but there were tracks below the pitch.... They were getting down with reasonable speed. Matt was going first. As he rounded a corner of the rock and looked down, all his fears dissolved: he saw the familiar orange tent and my head sticking out of it. He shouted a cheery hello, but I seemed not to have heard it in the wind. Don came in sight, then, and shouted another greeting. Again, I didn't answer. Matt was almost down to the tent. My silence seemed a bit peculiar, but surely—then he looked at the snow platform beside the tent, and saw that there was only one pack.

They took it bravely. They could understand the accident even less well than I. I had been afraid to tell them, but I leaned on them now, and they took the weight of my shock and helped me hold it.

We crowded together again and spent the night in the tent. The next day the storm increased. Around 7 P.M. we decided to complete the descent. We thought it should take about two more hours. It actually took eight.

The moment we got outside the tent, the whipping wind numbed us. We had a great deal of trouble chopping out the tent, and at last ripped out the corner of it. We had only one rope for the three of us, which made using the fixed ropes terribly clumsy. Matt had only one crampon, so he went in the middle. We tried placing him at various places along the rope, but none worked smoothly.

The conditions were hideous. A layer of new snow slid treacherously off the old ice. It grew dark quickly. We were shivering constantly, and had to shout at the tops of our voices to hear each other. Soon we couldn't even see the slope at our feet. We had to follow the ice-coated fixed ropes by feel, pulling them out of the crusted snow. I felt a continual dread of the sheer drop beneath us. We had three falls on the way down, but managed to catch each one with the fixed ropes.

It was the worst, most frightening climbing I have ever done. At last, in the early morning, we reached the last rappel. We slid down the ropes, out of the fierce gale to the blessedly flat, safe glacier below. Then we pulled down the rappel rope, cutting ourselves off for good from our route, from the summit, from the long, wonderful days of climbing, from Ed. We trudged back to our snow cave. Five days later Don Sheldon flew us out.

Thus an accident that made no sense, except in some trivial, mechanical way, robbed us suddenly of Ed, and of most of the joy of our accomplishment. Don, Matt, and I are left instead with a wilderness of emotions, with memories that blur too quickly of a friend who died too young. The shock and fear we lived with during the last days of our expedition all too easily now obscure the bright image of one perfect day—the summit day—when we seemed to work flawlessly together. Should we have found a safer way to become friends? Perhaps we could not. Perhaps the risk itself was what it took to bind us.

## Topics for Discussion and Writing

1. After the first accident, Roberts says that "The world seemed achingly beautiful, now that we had been reprieved to see it a while longer." Explain why a near disaster like this can make something, some place, even more beautiful.

2. "We were inexpressibly happy to be together," Roberts writes as the four climbers near the summit of Mount Huntington. Explain how reaching the top of a mountain can deepen the friendship between people. Does Roberts give any reason for this?

3. Have you ever done something dangerous, something risky, that made you feel especially close to another person? Write a narrative about this experience, and explain how risk works to bring people together.

4. How does Roberts react to the death of his friend Ed? Does this loss make him want to give up the activity of mountain climbing? Explain this reaction.

# A Country of Edges
### (1971)

## Wendell Berry

It is a country of overtowering edges. Again and again, walking down from the wooded ridgetops above the Red River Gorge one comes into the sound of water falling—the steady pouring and spattering of a tiny stream that has reached its grand occasion. And then one arrives at a great shady scoop in the cliff where the trail bends and steps and skids down to the foot of the fall. One looks up twenty or thirty or fifty or more feet to where the water leaps off the rock lip, catching the sunlight as it falls. Maybe there will be a rainbow in the spray. The trail may have passed through little shelves or terraces covered with wild iris in bloom. Or along the streamsides below the falls there may be pink lady's slippers. The slopes will be thickly shrubbed with rhododendron, darkened by the heavy green shade of hemlocks. And always on the wet faces of the rock there will be liverwort and meadow rue and mosses and ferns.

These places are as fresh, and they stay as fresh in the memory, as a clear, cold drink of water. They have a way of making me thirsty, whether I need a drink or not, and I like to hunt out a pool among the rocks and drink. The water is clean and cold. It is what water ought to be, for here one gets it "high and original," uncorrupted by any scientific miracle. There will be a clean gravelly bottom to the pool and its edges will bear the delicate garden-growth of the wet woods. There are the enclosing sounds of the water falling, and the voices of the phoebes and the Carolina wrens that nest in the sheltered places of the cliffs. Looking and listening are as important as tasting. One drinks in the sense of being in a good place.

The critical fact about water, wherever you find it in the Red River Gorge, is motion. Moving, it is gathering. All the little seeps and trickles of the slopes, the tiny streams heading up near the ridgetops and leaping and tumbling down the steep ravines—all are moving toward their union in the river.

And in the movement of its waters the place also is in motion; not to the human eye, nor to the collective vision of human history, but within the long gaze of geologic time the Gorge is moving within itself, deepening, changing the outline of its slopes; the river is growing into it like a great tree, steadily incising its branches into the land. For however gentle it may appear at certain seasons, this network of water known in sum as the Red River moves in its rocky notches as abrasive as a file.

How the river works as maker of the landscape, sculptor, arm of creation will always remain to some degree unknown, for it works with immeasurable leisure and patience, and often it works in turmoil. Although its processes may be hypothesized very convincingly, every vantage point of the country is also a point of speculation, a point of departure from the present surface into the shadowy questions of origin and of process.

By what complex interaction of flowing water, of weather, of growth and decay was that cliff given its shape? Where did this house-sized boulder fall from, what manner of sledging and breaking did it do coming down, what effect has it had on the course of the stream? What is happening now in all the swirling rapids and falls and eddies and pools of the river in flood? We know the results. But because we have not a thousand years to sit and watch, because our perspective is not that of birds or fish or of the lichens on the cliff face but only of men, because the life of the Gorge has larger boundaries than the life of a man, we know little of the processes.

To come to any understanding of the Red River one

must consider how minute and manifold are its workings, how far beyond count its lives and aspects and manifestations. But one must also sense its great power and its vastness. One must see in it the motive force of a landscape, the formal energy of all the country that drains into it. And one must stand on its banks aware that its life and meaning are not merely local but are intricately involved in all life and all meaning. It belongs to a family of rivers whose gathering will finally bring its water to mingle with the waters of the Yellowstone and the Kanahwa and the ocean. Its life belongs within—is dependent upon and to some extent necessary to—the life of the planet.

And so in the aspect of the river, in any of its moods, there is always a residual mystery. In its being it is too small and too large, too complex and too simple, too powerful and too delicate, too transient and too ancient and durable ever to be comprehended within the limits of a human life.

On the last Saturday in March we set out from Fletcher Ridge to walk down Mariba Fork, Laurel Fork, and Gladie Creek to the river. Last weekend there was deep snow. This morning it is sunny and warm. We walk past an old house site on the ridge—the clearing now grown up in thicket, the ground still covered with the dooryard periwinkles—and then down a steep path through the cliffs. As we approach the stream at the foot of the slope we begin to find hepaticas in bloom. They are everywhere, standing up in bright jaunty clumps like Sunday bouquets beneath the big poplars and beeches and hemlocks, and on the tops of boulders.

The path fades out. We follow the rocky edges of the stream, descending with the water gradually deeper into the land. As along all the streams of the Gorge, the country is divided by stones or cliffs or trees into distinct enclosures, a series of rooms, each one different in light and look and feeling from all the rest.

We find other flowers in bloom: trout lilies, rue anemones, trailing arbutus with its delicately scented blossoms almost hidden among the dead leaves. But running through all that day like an insistent, endlessly varied theme in a piece of music are the little gardens of hepaticas. Climbing onto a streamside terrace or entering the mouth of a ravine, we find the ground suddenly rich with them, the flowers a deep blue or lavender or pink or white. They are like Easter gone wild and hiding in the woods.

Downstream from where we camp that night we can see the rocky point of a cliff, high up, with a dead tree standing alone on it. And at twilight a pair of pileated woodpeckers cast off from that tree and make a long steep descent into the woods below, their flight powerful and somehow abandoned, joyous, accepting of the night.

Our walk ends the next day in the midst of a violent

downpour. We know that, behind us, the country we have passed through is changing. Its maker has returned to it yet again to do new work.

Flowing muddy and full, frothing over its rapids, its great sound filling the valley to the brim, the river is inscrutable and forbidding. The mind turns away from it, craving dry land like a frightened swimmer. The river will not stay still to be regarded or thought about. Its events are too much part of the flow, melting rapidly into one another, drawn on by the singular demand of the current.

Other times when the river is low, idling in its pools, its mysteries become inviting. One's thoughts eagerly leave solid ground then and take to the water. The current has ceased to be a threat and become an invitation. The thought of a boat comes to mind unasked and makes itself at home.

At such a time, a bright morning in early June, a canoe seems as satisfying and liberating as a pair of wings. One is empowered to pass beyond the shore, to follow the current that, other times, standing on the shore, one has merely wished to follow.

We wake at dawn, camped high on one of the ridges. Below us the hollows are drifted deep in white mist. While we eat breakfast and pack up we watch the mist shift with the stirrings of the air, rising, thickening and then thinning out, opening here and there so that we can see through to the treetops below, and closing again. It is as if the whole landscape is moving with a gentle dreaming motion. And then we drive down the windings of Highway 715, through the rapidly thinning mist, to the river. And now our canoe lies on the water in the shade-dappled weak light of the early morning. We have the day and the river before us.

Through the morning we paddle or drift through the long pools, idling with the river, stopping to look wherever our curiosity is tempted. We see a kingfisher, a water thrush, a Kentucky warbler, a muskrat, a snake asleep on an old tire caught on a snag, a lot of big, fat tadpoles three or four inches long, dragonflies with brilliant green bodies and black wings. In the clear shoals we see fish, and at intervals we pass the camps of fishermen, places their minds will turn back to, homesick, out of the confinement of winter and city and job. These are usually quiet and deserted; we have already passed the fishermen, fishing from the top of a boulder upstream, or we will find them in a boat a little way below.

On the bar at the mouth of Wolfpen Creek, where we stop for lunch, we watch several black and yellow swallow-tail butterflies drinking together on a spot of damp sand. They are like a bouquet of flowers that occasionally fly away and return again.

Where the swift clear water of Wolfpen enters the river a school of minnows is feeding. They work up the current over a little shoal of rippled sand, and then release themselves into the flow, drifting down through the quick water shadows to start again.

And all along the stream are boulders as big as houses that have broken from the cliffs and tumbled down. They are splotched with gray lichens and with mosses and liverworts; where enough dirt has collected in cracks and depressions in the stone there will be clumps of ferns or meadow rue or little patches of bluets. Above the high water line, where the current cannot sweep them, the long drama of soil-building has taken place on the tops of some of these rocks, so that they are now covered with plants and trees, and their surfaces look much like the surrounding forest floor. Those within reach of the floods are cleaner and more stony looking. They are not to be imperceptibly eaten away by the acids of the decay of vegetation and by the prizing of root and frost; they are being hewed out like sculptures by the direct violence of the river. Those that stand in the stream have been undercut by the steady abrasion of the current so that they rise out of the water like mushrooms. Going by them, one thinks of the thousands of miles of water that have flowed past them, and of the generations of boatmen, Indians and white men, that have paddled around them or stopped to fish in their shadows—and one feels their great weight and their silence and endurance. In the slanting light of the early morning the reflections off the water waver and flicker along their sides, the light moving over them with the movement of water.

There is no river more intimate with its banks. Everywhere the shore rises up steeply from the water like a page offered to be read. Water-borne, one seems always within arm's reach of the land. One has a walker's intimacy with the animals and plants of the shore as well as a boat-man's intimacy with the life of the water. Without rising from one's seat in the canoe one looks into the mossy cup of a phoebe's nest fastened to the rock and sees the five white eggs.

At intervals through the day we tense and focus our-selves as the river does, and move down into the head of a rapid. We pass through carefully, no longer paddling as we wish but as we must, following the main current as it bends through the rocks and the grassy shoals. And then we enter the quiet water of the pool below. Ahead of us a leaf falls from high up in a long gentle fall. In the water its reflection rises perfectly to meet it.

## Topics for Discussion and Writing

1. Examine this essay's five-part structure, and explain how the various sections fit together. How does this pattern of organization—general description of place; description of one characteristic (moving water); abstract meditation on the process of erosion; personal narrative; and more meditation framed within another narrative—fit the subject matter?

2. An "edge" is a sort of border, a place where various things make contact with each other. Why does Berry call his essay "A Country of Edges"? What sorts of connections occur in the essay?

3. Choose one of your favorite places and write a celebratory essay about it. Write about any place you want—a garden, a store, your home, a place in the mountains—but try to include at least one specific story (narrative), descriptions of specific physical objects, and some abstract explanation of natural processes and/or the workings of your own mind.

4. Look for specific images in Berry's essay that suggest the author's steadily increasing "intimacy" with this place. What sort of "advice" does the essay provide for readers who may also wish to achieve deep contact with places of their own?

# Walking
(1990)

## Linda Hogan

It began in dark and underground weather, a slow hunger moving toward light. It grew in a dry gully beside the road where I live, a place where entire hillsides are sometimes yellow, windblown tides of sunflower plants. But this one was different. It was alone, and larger than the countless others who had established their lives further up the hill. This one was a traveler, a settler, and like a dream beginning in conflict, it grew where the land had been disturbed.

I saw it first in early summer. It was a green and sleeping bud, raising itself toward the sun. Ants worked around the unopened bloom, gathering aphids and sap. A few days later, it was a tender young flower, soft and new, with a pale green center and a troop of silver gray insects climbing up and down the stalk.

Over the summer this sunflower grew into a plant of incredible beauty, turning its face daily toward the sun in the most subtle of ways, the black center of it dark and alive with a deep blue light, as if flint had sparked an elemental fire there, in community with rain, mineral, mountain air, and sand.

As summer changed from green to yellow there were new visitors daily: the lace-winged insects, the bees whose legs were fat with pollen, and grasshoppers with their clattering wings and desperate hunger. There were other lives I missed, lives too small or hidden to see. It was as if this plant with its host of lives was a society, one in which moment by moment, depending on light and moisture, there was great and diverse change.

There were changes in the next larger world around the plant as well. One day I rounded a bend in the road to find the disturbing sight of a dead horse, black and still against a hillside, eyes rolled back. Another day I was nearly lifted by a wind and sandstorm so fierce and hot that I had to wait for it to pass before I could return home. On this day the faded dry petals of the sunflower were swept across the land. That was when the birds arrived to carry the new seeds to another future.

In this one plant, in one summer season, a drama of need and survival took place. Hungers were filled. Insects coupled. There was escape, exhaustion, and death. Lives touched down a moment and were gone.

I was an outsider. I only watched. I never learned the sunflower's golden language or the tongues of its citizens. I had a small understanding, nothing more than a shallow observation of the flower, insects, and birds. But they knew what to do, how to live. An old voice from somewhere, gene or cell, told the plant how to evade the pull of gravity and find its way upward, how to open. It was instinct, intuition, necessity. A certain knowing directed the seed-bearing birds on paths to ancestral homelands they had never seen. They believed it. They followed.

There are other summons and calls, some even more mysterious than those commandments to birds or those survival journeys of insects. In bamboo plants, for instance, with their thin green canopy of light and golden stalks that creak in the wind. Once a century, all of a certain kind of bamboo flower on the same day. Whether they are in Malaysia or in a greenhouse in Minnesota makes no difference, nor does the age or size of the plant. They flower. Some current of an inner language passes between them, through space and separation, in ways we cannot explain in our language. They are all, somehow, one plant, each with a share of communal knowledge.

John Hay, in *The Immortal Wilderness*, has written: "There are occasions when you can hear the mysterious language of the Earth, in water, or coming through the trees, emanating from the mosses, seeping through the undercurrents of the soil, but you have to be willing to wait and receive."

Sometimes I hear it talking. The light of the sunflower was one language, but there are others, more audible. Once, in the redwood forest, I heard a beat, something like a drum or heart coming from the ground and trees and wind. That underground current stirred a kind of knowing inside me, a kinship and longing, a dream barely remembered that disappeared back to the body.

Another time, there was the booming voice of an ocean storm thundering from far out at sea, telling about what lived in the distance, about the rough water that would arrive, wave after wave revealing the disturbance at center.

Tonight I walk. I am watching the sky. I think of the people who came before me and how they knew the placement of stars in the sky, watched the moving sun long and hard enough to witness how a certain angle of light touched a stone only once a year. Without written records, they knew the gods of every night, the small, fine details of the world around them and of immensity above them.

Walking, I can almost hear the redwoods beating. And the oceans are above me here, rolling clouds, heavy and dark, considering snow. On the dry, red road, I pass the place of the sunflower, that dark and secret location where creation took place. I wonder if it will return this summer, if it will multiply and move up to the other stand of flowers in a territorial struggle.

It's winter and there is smoke from the fires. The square, lighted windows of houses are fogging over. It is a world of elemental attention, of all things working together, listening to what speaks in the blood. Whichever road I follow, I walk in the land of many gods, and they love and eat one another.

Walking, I am listening to a deeper way. Suddenly all my ancestors are behind me. Be still, they say. Watch and listen. You are the result of the love of thousands.

## Topics for Discussion and Writing

1. Although Hogan calls her essay "Walking," this piece is clearly concerned with more than the activity of putting one foot in front of the other. What else is Hogan doing besides moving from place to place? How are her senses —like sight and hearing—involved?

2. What does it mean to "hear the mysterious language of the Earth"? Why does Hogan think it is valuable to listen for the planet "talking"?

3. At the end of the essay, Hogan says that her "ancestors are behind" her. Because the author is a Native American, she feels an ancient bond with the land. Is it possible even for non-Native people to be so attentive and respectful?

4. Write a narrative of one of your own recent walks, imitating the style of Hogan's essay. Notice how her essay begins with detailed, physical description but moves on to present a deeper, more spiritual response to nature. Try, in your own essay, to describe (or imagine) "a world of elemental attention."

# Freedom and Wilderness, Wilderness and Freedom
### (1977)

## Edward Abbey

When I lived in Hoboken, just across the lacquered Hudson from Manhattan, we had all the wilderness we needed. There was the waterfront with its decaying piers and abandoned warehouses, the jungle of bars along River Street and Hudson Street, the houseboats, the old ferry slips, the mildew-green cathedral of the Erie-Lackawanna Railway terminal. That was back in 1964-65: then came Urban Renewal, which ruined everything left lovable in Hoboken, New Jersey.

What else was there? I loved the fens, those tawny marshes full of waterbirds, mosquitoes, muskrats, and opossums that intervened among the black basaltic rocks between Jersey City and Newark, and somewhere back of Union City on the way to gay, exotic, sausage-packing, garbage-rich Secaucus. I loved also and finally and absolute-

ly, as a writer must love any vision of eschatological ulti-
mates, the view by twilight from the Pulaski Skyway (Stop
for Emergency Repairs Only) of the Seventh Circle of Hell.
Those melancholy chemical plants, ancient as acid, sick as
cyanide, rising beyond the cattails and tules; the gleam of
oily waters in the refineries' red glare; the desolation of the
endless, incomprehensible uninhabitable (but inhabited)
slums of Harrison, Newark, Elizabeth; the haunting and
sinister odors on the wind. Rust and iron and sunflowers in
the tangled tracks, the great grimy sunsets beyond the satu-
rated sky.... It will all be made, someday, a national park of
the mind, a rigid celebration of industrialism's finest frenzy.

We tried north too, up once into the Catskills, once
again to the fringe of the Adirondacks. All I saw were
Private Property Keep Out This Means You signs. I live in a
different country now. Those days of longing, that experi-
ment in exile, are all past. The far-ranging cat returns at last
to his natural, native habitat. But what wilderness there was
in those bitter days I learned to treasure. Foggy nights in
greasy Hoboken alleyways kept my soul alert, healthy and
aggressive, on edge with delight.

The other kind of wilderness is also useful. I mean now
the hardwood forests of upper Appalachia, the overrated
mountains of Colorado, the burnt sienna hills of South
Dakota, the raw umber of Kansas, the mysterious swamps
of Arkansas, the porphyritic mountains of purple Arizona,

the mystic desert of my own four-cornered country—this and 347 other good, clean, dangerous places I could name.

Science is not sufficient. "Ecology" is a word I first read in H. G. Wells twenty years ago and I still don't know what it means. Or seriously much care. Nor am I primarily concerned with nature as living museum, the preservation of spontaneous plants and wild animals. The wildest animal I know is you, gentle reader, with this helpless book clutched in your claws. No, there are better reasons for keeping the wild wild, the wilderness open, the trees up and the rivers free, and the canyons uncluttered with dams.

We need wilderness because we are wild animals. Every man needs a place where he can go to go crazy in peace. Every Boy Scout troop deserves a forest to get lost, miserable, and starving in. Even the maddest murderer of the sweetest wife should get a chance for a run to the sanctuary of the hills. If only for the sport of it. For the terror, freedom, and delirium. Because we need brutality and raw adventure, because men and women first learned to love in, under, and all around trees, because we need for every pair of feet and legs about ten leagues of naked nature, crags to leap from, mountains to measure by, deserts to finally die in when the heart fails.

The prisoners in Solzhenitsyn's labor camps looked out on the vast Siberian forests—within those shadowy depths lay the hope of escape, of refuge, of survival, of hope itself

—but guns and barbed wire blocked the way. The citizens of our American cities enjoy a high relative degree of political, intellectual, and economic liberty; but if the entire nation is urbanized, industrialized, mechanized, and administered, then our liberties continue only at the sufferance of the technological megamachine that functions both as servant and master, and our freedoms depend on the pleasure of the privileged few who sit at the control consoles of that machine. What makes life in our cities at once still tolerable, exciting, and stimulating is the existence of an alternative option, whether exercised or not, whether even appreciated or not, of a radically different mode of being *out there,* in the forests, on the lakes and rivers, in the deserts, up in the mountains.

Who needs wilderness? Civilization needs wilderness. The idea of wilderness preservation is one of the fruits of civilization, like Bach's music, Tolstoy's novels, scientific medicine, novocaine, space travel, free love, the double martini, the secret ballot, the private home and private property, the public park and public property, freedom of travel, the Bill of Rights, peppermint toothpaste, beaches for nude bathing, the right to own and bear arms, the right not to own and bear arms, and a thousand other good things one could name, some of them trivial, most of them essential, all of them vital to that great, bubbling, disorderly, anarchic, unmanageable diversity of opinion, expression, and ways of living which free men and women love, which is their breath of life, and which the authoritarians of church and state and war and sometimes even art despise and always have despised. And feared.

The permissive society? What else? I love America because it *is* a confused, chaotic mess—and I hope we can keep it this way for at least another thousand years. The permissive society is the free society, the open society. Who gave us permission to live this way? Nobody did. *We* did. And that's the way it should be—only more so. The best cure for the ills of democracy is more democracy.

The boundary around a wilderness area may well be an artificial, self-imposed, sophisticated construction, but once inside that line you discover the artificiality beginning to drop away; and the deeper you go, the longer you stay, the more interesting things get—sometimes fatally interesting. And that too is what we want: Wilderness is and should be a place where, as in Central Park, New York City, you have a fair chance of being mugged and buggered by a shaggy fellow in a fur coat—one of Pooh Bear's big brothers. To be alive is to take risks; to be always safe and secure is death.

Enough of these banalities—no less true anyhow—which most of us embrace. But before getting into the practical applications of this theme, I want to revive one more argument for the preservation of wilderness, one seldom heard but always present, in my own mind at least, and that is the political argument.

Democracy has always been a rare and fragile institution in human history. Never was it more in danger than now, in the dying decades of this most dangerous of centuries. Within the past few years alone we have seen two more relatively open societies succumb to dictatorship and police rule—Chile and India. In all of Asia there is not a single free country except Israel—which, as the Arabs say, is really a transplanted piece of Europe. In Africa, obviously going the way of Latin America, there are none. Half of Europe stagnates under one-man or one-party domination. Only Western Europe and Britain, Australia and New Zealand, perhaps Japan, and North America can still be called more or less free, open, democratic societies.

As I see it, our own nation is not free from the danger of dictatorship. And I refer to internal as well as external threats to our liberties. As social conflict tends to become more severe in this country—and it will unless we strive for social justice—there will inevitably be a tendency on the part of the authoritarian element—always present in our history—to suppress individual freedoms, to utilize the refined techniques of police surveillance (not excluding torture, of course) in order to preserve—not wilderness! —but the status quo, the privileged positions of those who now so largely control the economic and governmental institutions of the United States.

If this fantasy should become reality—and fantasies becoming realities are the story of the twentieth century—then some of us may need what little wilderness remains as a place of refuge, as a hideout, as a base from which to carry on guerrilla warfare against the totalitarianism of my nightmares. I hope it does not happen; I believe we will prevent it from happening; but if it should, then I, for one, intend to light out at once for the nearest national forest, where I've been hiding cases of peanut butter, home-brew, ammunition, and C-rations for the last ten years. I haven't the slightest doubt that the FBI, the NSA, the CIA, and the local cops have dossiers on me a yard thick. If they didn't, I'd be insulted. Could I survive in the wilderness? I don't know—but I do know I could never survive in prison.

Could we as a people survive without wilderness? To consider that question we might look at the history of modern Europe, and of other places. As the Europeans filled up their small continent, the more lively among them spread out over the entire planet, seeking fortune, empire, a new world, a new chance—but seeking most of all, I believe, for adventure, for the opportunity of self- testing. Those nations that were confined by geography, bottled up, tended to find their outlet for surplus energy through war on their neighbors; the Germans provide the best example of this thesis. Nations with plenty of room for expansion, such as the Russians, tended to be less aggressive toward their neighbors.

In Asia we can see the same human necessities at work in somewhat different forms. Japan might be likened to Germany; a small nation with a large, ever-growing, vigorous, and intelligent population. Confined by the sea, their open spaces long ago occupied and domesticated, the Japanese like the Germans turned to war upon their neighbors, particularly China, Korea, and Oriental Russia; and when that was not enough to fully engage their surplus energies, they became an oceanic power, which soon brought them into conflict with two other oceanic powers— Britain and the United States. Defeated in war, the Japanese turned their undefeated energies into industry and commerce, becoming a world power through trade. But that kind of adventure is satisfactory for only a small part of the population; and when the newly prosperous Japanese middle class becomes bored with tourism, we shall probably see some kind of civil war or revolution in Japan—perhaps within the next twenty years.

Something of that sort may be said to have already happened in China. Powerless to wage war upon their neighbors, the Chinese waged war upon themselves, class against class, the result a triumphant revolution and the construction of a human society that may well become, unfortunately, the working model for all. I mean the thoroughly organized society, where all individual freedom is submerged to the needs of the social organism.

The global village and the technological termitarium. More nightmares! I do not believe that human beings would or could long tolerate such a world. The human animal is almost infinitely adaptable—but there must be limits to our adaptability, limits beyond which, if we can survive them at all, we would survive only by sacrificing those qualities that distinguish the human from that possible cousin of the future: the two-legged, flesh-skinned robot, his head, her head, its head wired by telepathic radio to a universal central control system.

One more example: What happened to India when its space was filled, its wilderness destroyed? Something curiously different from events in Europe, China, or Japan; unable to expand outward in physical space, unable or unwilling (so far) to seek solutions through civil war and revolution, the genius of India—its most subtle and sensitive minds—sought escape from unbearable reality by rocket flights of thought into the inner space of the soul, into a mysticism so deep and profound that a whole nation, a whole people, have been paralyzed for a thousand years by awe and adoration.

Now we see something similar happening in our own country. A tiny minority, the technological elite, blast off for the moon, continuing the traditional European drive for the conquest of physical space. But a far greater number, lacking the privileges and luck and abilities of the Glenns and the Armstrongs and their comrades, have attempted to imitate the way of India: When reality becomes intolerable, when the fantasies of nightmare become everyday experience, then deny that reality, obliterate it, and escape, escape, escape, through drugs, through trance and enchantment, through magic and madness, or through study and discipline. By whatever means, in some cases by *any* means, escape this crazy, unbearable, absurd playpen of the senses —this gross 3-D, grade-B, X-rated, porno flick thrust upon us by CBS News, *Time, Newsweek*, the *New York Times*, *Rolling Stone*, and the *Sierra Club Bulletin*—seeking refuge in a nicer universe just next door, around some corner of the mind and nervous system, deep in the coolest cells of the brain. If all is illusion then nothing matters, or matters much; and if nothing matters then peace, of a sort, is possible, striving becomes foolish, and we can finally relax, at last, into that bliss which passeth understanding, content as pigs on a warm manure pile. Until the man comes with the knife, to carry the analogy to its conclusion, until pig-sticking time rolls around again and the fires are lit under the scalding tubs.

You begin to see the outline of my obsessions. Every train of thought seems to lead to some concentration camp of nightmare. But I believe there are alternatives to the world of nightmare. I believe that there are better ways to live than the traditional European-American drive for power, conquest, domination; better ways than the horrifying busyness of the Japanese; better ways than the totalitarian communes of the Chinese; better ways than the passive pipe dreams of Hindu India, that sickliest of all nations.

I believe we can find models for a better way both in the past and the present. Imperfect models, to be sure, each with its grievous faults, but better all the same than most of what passes for necessity in the modern world. I allude to the independent city-states of classical Greece; to the free cities of medieval Europe; to the small towns of eighteenth- and nineteenth-century America; to the tribal life of the American Plains Indians; to the ancient Chinese villages recalled by Lao-tse in his book, *The Way*.

I believe it is possible to find and live a balanced way of life somewhere halfway between all-out industrialism on the one hand and a make-believe pastoral idyll on the other. I believe it possible to live an intelligent life in our cities—if we make them fit to live in—if we stop this trend toward joining city unto city until half the nation and half the planet becomes one smog-shrouded, desperate and sweating, insane and explosive urbanized concentration camp.

According to my basic thesis, if it's sound, we can avoid the disasters of war, the nightmare of the police state and totalitarianism, the drive to expand and conquer, if we return to this middle way and learn to live for a while, say at least a thousand years or so, just for the hell of it, just for the fun of it, in some sort of steady-state economy, some sort of free, democratic, wide-open society.

As we return to a happier equilibrium between industrialism and a rural-agrarian way of life, we will of course also encourage a gradual reduction of the human population of these states to something closer to the optimum: perhaps half the present number. This would be accomplished by humane social policies, naturally, by economic and taxation incentives encouraging birth control, the single-child family, the unmarried state, the community family. Much preferable to war, disease, revolution, nuclear poisoning, etc., as population control devices.

What has all this fantasizing to do with wilderness and freedom? We can have wilderness without freedom; we can have wilderness without human life at all; but we cannot have freedom without wilderness, we cannot have freedom without leagues of open space beyond the cities, where boys and girls, men and women, can live at least part of their lives under no control but their own desires and abilities, free from any and all direct administration by their fellow men. "A world without wilderness is a cage," as Dave Brower says.

I see the preservation of wilderness as one sector of the front in the war against the encroaching industrial state.

Every square mile of range and desert saved from the strip miners, every river saved from the dam builders, every forest saved from the loggers, every swamp saved from the land speculators means another square mile saved for the play of human freedom.

All this may seem utopian, impossibly idealistic. No matter. There comes a point at every crisis in human affairs when the ideal must become the real—or nothing. It is my contention that if we wish to save what is good in our lives and give our children a taste of a good life, we must bring a halt to the ever-expanding economy and put the growth maniacs under medical care.

Let me tell you a story.

A couple of years ago I had a job I worked for an outfit called Defenders of Fur Bearers (now known as Defenders of Wildlife). I was caretaker and head janitor of a 70,000-acre wildlife refuge in the vicinity of Aravaipa Canyon in southern Arizona. The Whittell Wildlife Preserve, as we called it, was a refuge for mountain lion, javelina, a few black bear, maybe a wolf or two, a herd of whitetail deer, and me, to name the principal fur bearers.

I was walking along Aravaipa Creek one afternoon when I noticed fresh mountain lion tracks leading ahead of me. Big tracks, the biggest lion tracks I've seen anywhere. Now I've lived most of my life in the Southwest, but I am sorry to admit that I had never seen a mountain lion in the wild. Naturally I was eager to get a glimpse of this one.

It was getting late in the day, the sun already down beyond the canyon wall, so I hurried along, hoping I might catch up to the lion and get one good look at him before I had to turn back and head home. But no matter how fast I walked and then jogged along, I couldn't seem to get any closer; those big tracks kept leading ahead of me, looking not five minutes old, but always disappearing around the next turn in the canyon.

Twilight settled in, visibility getting poor. I realized I'd have to call it quits. I stopped for a while, staring upstream into the gloom of the canyon. I could see the buzzards settling down for the evening in their favorite dead cottonwood. I heard the poor-wills and the spotted toads beginning to sing, but of that mountain lion I could neither hear nor see any living trace.

I turned around and started home. I'd walked maybe a mile when I thought I heard something odd behind me. I stopped and looked back—nothing; nothing but the canyon, the running water, the trees, the rocks, the willow thickets. I went on and soon I heard that noise again—the sound of footsteps.

I stopped. The noise stopped. Feeling a bit uncomfortable now—it was getting dark—with all the ancient superstitions of the night starting to crawl from the crannies of my soul, I looked back again.

And this time I saw him. About fifty yards behind me, poised on a sand bar, one front paw still lifted and waiting, stood this big cat, looking straight at me. I could see the gleam of the twilight in his eyes. I was startled as always by how small a cougar's head seems but how long and lean and powerful the body really is. To me, at that moment, he looked like the biggest cat in the world. He looked dangerous. Now I know very well that mountain lions are supposed almost never to attack human beings. I knew there was nothing to fear—but I couldn't help thinking maybe this lion is different from the others. Maybe he knows we're in a wildlife preserve, where lions can get away with anything. I was not unarmed; I had my Swiss army knife in my pocket with the built in can opener, the corkscrew, the two-inch folding blade, the screwdriver. Rationally there was nothing to fear; all the same I felt fear.

And something else too: I felt what I always feel when I meet a large animal face to face in the wild: I felt a kind of affection and the crazy desire to communicate, to make some kind of emotional, even physical contact with the animal. After we'd stared at each other for maybe five seconds —it seemed at the time like five minutes—I held out one hand and took a step toward the big cat and said something ridiculous like, "Here, kitty, kitty." The cat paused there on three legs, one paw up as if he wanted to shake hands. But he didn't respond to my advance.

I took a second step toward the lion. Again the lion remained still, not moving a muscle, not blinking an eye. And I stopped and thought again and this time I understood that however the big cat might secretly feel, I myself was not yet quite ready to shake hands with a mountain lion. Maybe someday. But not yet. I retreated.

I turned and walked homeward again, pausing every few steps to look back over my shoulder. The cat had lowered his front paw but did not follow me. The last I saw of him, from the next bend of the canyon, he was still in the same place, watching me go. I hurried on through the evening, stopping now and then to look and listen, but if that cat followed me any further I could detect no sight or sound of it.

I haven't seen a mountain lion since that evening, but the experience remains shining in my memory. I want my children to have the opportunity for that kind of experience. I want my friends to have it. I want even our enemies to have it—they need it most. And someday, possibly, one of our children's children will discover how to get close enough to that mountain lion to shake paws with it, to embrace and caress it, maybe even teach it something, and to learn what the lion has to teach us.

## Topics for Discussion and Writing

1. According to Abbey, "We need wilderness because we are wild animals." What does he mean by this? Is this true about sophisticated, city people, too?

2. A "wilderness," for Abbey, is a place of splendid, life-enriching danger. Compare Abbey's notion of risk with David Roberts's example in "Five Days on Mount Huntington."

3. Abbey quotes David Brower, the longtime director of the Sierra Club (a major American conservationist organization), as saying, "A world without wilderness is a cage." Read carefully through the lengthy statement in middle of the essay about wilderness and freedom. Why do we need wilderness if we want free, democratic societies? Write an essay in which you examine Abbey's claims about wilderness and freedom, applying them to life in contemporary Japan.

4. Look at the "story" Abbey tells at the end of his essay about meeting a cougar (puma) in the Arizona desert. Expain, either in class discussion or in a paper, how this story demonstrates the central ideas of Abbey's essay.

# The Third Eye of the Lizard
(1993)

## Ray Gonzalez

ॐ

I killed hundreds of lizards when I was a boy. I shot them with my BB gun because it was a favorite sport for my friends and me. Shooting lizards helped to relieve the monotony of living in a small desert town. In 1963 my parents' house was built in a newly developed part of north-west El Paso. It sat on the outskirts of town, right in the middle of the desert, which meant that we were surround-ed by rattlesnakes and lizards, creatures uprooted from their natural habitat by the new housing developments.

The empty lots around the house were havens for tum-bleweeds and dozens of lizards. After a summer rain, I would walk through the lots, kick the weeds out of the way and watch the small gray and white lizards scatter for cover. I carried my loaded BB gun into the desert because I had a fantasy of shooting a huge rattlesnake, something that never happened. I killed many lizards without shame or guilt because I saw them as a threat to my life there, plus it was an ideal way to play out the timeless drama between the hunter and prey, the dance that begins when men are still boys.

Killing lizards became as routine as stepping on ants or swatting flies. There were endless numbers of lizards in the desert and many wandered into our yard, sunned themselves on the sidewalk, or crawled up the brick walls of the house. The most common was the collar lizard, four or five inches long, counting the tail. The creatures were lightning quick, but made good targets. When the lizards paused, they reared up on their hind legs and trembled.

It was the moment to shoot. To be effective, you needed to be at least ten feet close. (BB guns are not very accurate.) I often missed, the pellet springing dirt into the air as the pale lizard leaped away. When I got lucky and hit one, it would bounce into the air and land on its back, twitching, its white belly exposed to the sun. Then it would lie still.

During that moment, at the age of eleven, I felt powerful knowing I was a successful hunter—the conqueror, the proud killer, the triumphant American soldier, a favorite fantasy of young boys who dreamed beyond their big box of plastic toy soldiers. I grew up watching violent cartoons long before anyone cared to make an issue about the carnage kids were exposed to on TV. With my friends, I played "army" and owned a huge pile of toy guns. I even got a G.I. Joe the first year they were made in the early sixties. Getting my father to buy me a Daisy BB rifle was the next logical step. I had earned it by having many exciting adventures and fantasies as a neighborhood soldier, defending the long row of new houses against the dangers of living in the desert. By exterminating so many lizards, I kept the neighborhood safe. Dangers were tamed with my BB gun.

One summer I decided to keep track of how many lizards I killed by collecting their tails in a large matchbox. It had never occurred to me to count tails until the first time I encountered lizards shedding them. I cornered a small lizard in a cardboard box one day, and decided not to shoot it. I wanted a live one to exhibit in a glass jar I sometimes carried with me. Unafraid, I reached down to grab the tiny thing. As I touched the tail, it came off. I was so shocked, I dropped it. The tail shook by itself as the lizard ran out of the box. I had never seen a tail with a life of its own.

This reflexive self-dismemberment, or autotomy as it is called, is a widely-known phenomenon among scientists who study such things, but it is a real shocker the first time you discover it. I stopped hunting lizards for several days after that, thinking that some evil desert spirit was punishing me for killing so many. But my friends told me it was part of being a lizard—the tail came off naturally and the lizard would grow a new one. I got over my guilt and proceeded to grab the tails of any lizards I shot. The tails always fell off, to twitch in the matchbox. I don't recall how many I had in the box when it disappeared one day. My mother probably found it. She must have screamed at the decaying little tails and thrown them away.

For awhile, my friends and I wanted to see twitching tails more than dead lizards. Instead of using our BB guns, we started going after the lizards with sticks to cut the tails off. We fell for a lizard's natural defense. If the lizard is frightened enough, touching its body is enough to cause a detachment of the tail. The tail then wiggles strongly and attracts more attention than the lizard. The reptiles in my neighborhood must have realized it was better to leave their tails behind than to be blown away. Casualties went down when my friends and I stood around watching little tails shaking on the ground while the bare-assed lizard took off. We must have eventually caught on though; after the first summer of discovering detachable tails, we went back to shooting the lizards.

By the age of thirteen, after I discovered rock-and-roll music, I lost interest in guns and killing lizards forever. My last summer of killing them is memorable—my greatest challenge as a hunter came with the appearance of the biggest lizard I had ever seen in the neighborhood. This huge reptile so threatened my territory it made me carry extra BB pellets in the pockets of my torn Levi's.

I first saw it clinging to the back door that led into the garage. It was a fat, dark-brown lizard measuring a good ten inches. It was not a collar lizard. I first thought it was a Gila monster, but knew they didn't exist in Texas, only in the Sonora desert of Arizona. (I had looked that up in the school encyclopedia long ago.)

I grabbed my BB gun and fired the first shot from several yards away. I missed and heard the thunk of the pellet embedding itself in the wooden door. The huge lizard darted into a crevice between the roof of the house and the doorway. I was excited, but knew I should have gotten closer. Usually, I was a very patient hunter, and my friends always kidded me because I was the best marksman among us.

I saw it again a few days later. It lay along the edge of the concrete flower bed in the backyard. I stepped closer and fired from about six feet away. The shot ricocheted off the cement and the lizard flew off. I thought I hit it, but could find no trace of it in the flower box.

I did not see the mysterious, dark creature for over two weeks, until one day I walked past the garage door to find it near the same spot where it had first appeared. I aimed carefully and fired. I missed again and was stunned to see the lizard did not move or run. I quickly recocked the single-shot air rifle and fired a second time. The second pellet buried itself in the door with my other stray shots. The lizard fell with a thud and then ran under the door. It disappeared in a stack of firewood inside the garage.

I counted the BBs stuck in the door and couldn't believe the strange luck of this reptile. I went to the woodpile and kicked logs around until I heard a scraping sound underneath. The lizard was trapped, but I couldn't see it. I came back the next day, poked around and heard it. I wondered why it didn't run out the door. Maybe lizards with their reptilian brains were still not smart enough to find their way out of a room. I waited in the garage, but it didn't come out.

For five days I went into the garage without flushing it out. On the morning of the sixth day, as I crossed the backyard toward the garage, I saw the lizard sitting high on the brick wall of the house. It had finally made its move. I cocked the rifle, aimed, and slowly drew closer. I fired from a few feet away.

The lizard flew off the wall and landed behind two trash cans. It shivered for a few seconds, its large brown feet outstretched, its long, thick tail twitching slowly. Watching it die, I was suddenly afraid. This was the biggest thing I had killed. I felt panic and guilt I had never encountered before as a boy with a nasty BB gun. I was too shaken to bury the lizard or throw it into the trash can. I knew the ants would get it soon. (It was a common sight to walk through the desert and see red army ants picking clean the tiny skeletons of dead lizards.)

The day after I shot the big lizard, I came back to the trash cans to see what the ants had done. The lizard's thick body lay on its stomach. When I hit it, it had landed on its back. I wondered if ants had the power to turn it over.

Hundreds of them crawled over the body. They had eaten half of the right side around its belly. My shot had split its back, offering another entry for the carnivorous ants. What struck me that day was the sudden appearance of a rough, round band on top of the lizard's head. I bent over to study it closer. I had never seen such a design on a lizard. The circle on its head was a lighter brown, almost pale red, and looked like a marking you might find on a rattlesnake. As I gazed at the intricate colorings on the dead animal, the sense of dread and guilt returned. I walked away and did not check on the lizard for several days. When I came back, it was gone. The only trace was a dark spot of blood and the remains of a gnarled foot. Even the skeleton was gone.

Years later, I came across the key to the circle on the lizard's head. In his book *Desert Journal* (University of California, 1977), naturalist Raymond Cowles writes that some species of lizards have a third eye on top of their heads. He calls them parietal eyes and says researchers have found no mechanism for vision in the third eye. He feels the parietal eye in lizards helps regulate daily and seasonal exposure to sunlight, but there are theories some dinosaurs and ancient reptiles may have had a third eye once, a good extra eyeball for defense against approaching enemies.

In his essay "The Three Brains," poet Robert Bly speculates about which parts of ourselves have not truly evolved, and which parts of our brains remain reptilian. He speculates that we all have reptilian brains working to think about the need for food, survival, and security. Perhaps this is what made the lizard so elusive and mysterious, an unexplainable connection to both of our reptilian states. Did the lizard dodge so many of my BBs because it was watching me the whole time? Did I kill lizards because I wanted to survive in the desert without hidden eyes witnessing everything I did? Later in the essay, Bly announces that the desert landscape rarely contains mammal images. He feels that lizards and snakes dominate and influence the way we behave when we live in such arid places.

The lizard I killed had a third eye, and my memory of its head is an image that is reptilian, not mammalian. The third eye closes around the mysteries of the desert and how living in it is crucial to learning why we hide ourselves in our three brains. Its third eye made sure I recalled what I killed, why I keep going back to the memory of the huge lizard, why I spent so much time as the great hunter.

The fact I found the lizard's body was turned over the

day after I left it on its back, has something to do with the third eye. Perhaps, it made it easier for one last look at me. The third eye stood out from the decaying body the last time I saw it, a detail I missed until the final hunt. No other lizard I killed as a boy revealed a third eye to focus on me.

*　*　*

The big lizard was the last one I killed. Somehow, my need to be a hunter ended. I found my BB gun rusting in the garage the following summer. Eventually, my mother threw it away.

The holes in the garage door are still there. Some of them contain old BB pellets that have found their place in the wood like remnants of an old western shootout. A few years ago, while visiting my family, I walked around the house and spotted the holes in the door. As I counted fourteen holes, I tried to think of a reason why I had loved to shoot lizards. What made me do it? Many of my friends shot birds. A couple of them got into trouble for hurting cats and dogs with their BB guns. I never shot birds or any other animal besides lizards. Were lizards acceptable because they were so abundant in the area? Was it human fear of monsters coming to get me? I rarely see them anymore when I visit the desert.

Absence of Lizards

I haven't seen a lizard
since I left the desert,
though I feel a lizard
behind my eyelids.
It darts in and out,
though I can't see it,
can't really picture it
jumping off a rock
to sit inside my head.

I recall the invasion
of the white lizards,
the season they beat
the desert rain, overflowed
into the arroyos,
sat on the adobe walls
like cut-off fingers,
twitching their tails,
waiting for me to approach
before leaping into
the cactus like torn pieces
of paper I threw away,
white lizards flashing
their mocking dance at me.

The last giant lizard I saw
was shot by a kid with a BB gun.
It was a foot-long,
dark-brown, thick, and fast.
The kid was a good shot
and left it in the dirt lot
across from my house.
I found it on my walk,
ants crawling over the rocks
to get to it, hundreds of them
opening the stiff, pregnant body
to get to the yellow eggs that
spilled out of its belly like
kernels of corn fertilizing
the hot sand.

Writing this poem and finding the twenty-five-year-old holes in the door unlocked the most important detail about the elusive lizard I finally killed. I have several recurring dreams about growing up in the desert. Most of the dreams involve images of old adobe ruins and cliff dwellings— stretches of hot ground crawling with dozens of enormous rattlesnakes, some sleeping entangled in each other, some poised to strike at me. When I dream of snakes, I wake up with no fear or anxiety, but I also wake with the memory of the third eye on the lizard. Somewhere, the lizards I killed as a boy watch me as snakes surround me in my dreams, but the lizards don't show themselves. Perhaps, I tried to erase it from my soul by giving up my ways as a hunter with a BB gun.

What does that say about us as predators? Can we truly forget? The huge lizard may be waiting for me to join it as it scurries across a field of tumbleweeds, fresh ground after a summer rain when the desert opens and hundreds of lizards, large and small, flash their tails before the arrogant hunter.

**Topics for Discussion and Writing**

1. Why did Gonzalez enjoy hunting lizards as a young boy? Explain the author's childhood fascination with this activity.

2. When Gonzalez killed the "huge lizard" during his final summer of lizard hunting, at first he did not seem to feel any of the guilt, the moral uncertainty, that Lopez experiences as an adult who accidentally kills animals while driving. What sort of emotion did Gonzalez experience, though? Analyze the tone (the mood) of this scene.

3. The "third eye" of the dead lizard seems to continue watching the young Gonzalez even after the lizard is dead: "Its third eye made sure I recalled what I killed, why I keep going back to the memory of the huge lizard, why I spent so much time as the great hunter." The watching eye of the lizard may represent the writer's own conscience, the mysterious depths of his own brain. Discuss the parallels between the feelings of moral responsibility toward animals (toward the world in general) in Lopez's "Apologia" and Gonzalez's "The Third Eye of the Lizard."

4. Consider some childhood activity that now makes you feel guilty. Why did you do it? Why won't your mind let you forget it? Write an essay in which you tell the story of this experience and explain how this memory determines who you are as an adult. You may wish, like Gonzalez, to include a short poem about this memory in the midst of your essay.

# Wildness and Walls
(1993)

## John Elder

*

I traveled slowly toward Japan, through a landscape of literature, observing the beauty of each new season as it flowed into the life of the people. Lady Murasaki, in the eleventh-century *Tale of Genji*, slid open the door disclosing a garden of Heian courtiers. Her shining company played their flutes under the moon in time to the swaying of the bamboo. They dyed the bamboo of those flutes to match the green of the pines and dressed in the "wild aster combination" as fields around the palace gave way to magenta and green. Six centuries later, in the time of the shōguns, Bashō walked north toward the bay of Matsushima, "the pine islands." Looking over that world of wind-sculpted rock, of trees bent out over the thousand coves, he composed a haiku in which the Japanese name gusted into the rush of water, of wind:

*Matsushima ya*
*aa matsushima ya*
*matsushima ya*

The more I read, the more I wanted to follow Japan's testimonies of natural freshness back to the landscape of their origin, to experience a sensitivity to the earth transcending the dichotomies of the American wilderness movement. The American system of national parks, culminating in the Wilderness Act of 1964, had made a unique contribution to the stewardship of nature in the twentieth century. But it had also contributed in certain ways to the polarization of "nature" and "culture." At any rate, that phase of our environmental evolution seemed to have come to an end with the passage of the Alaska Lands Bill in 1980. I wondered whether the Japanese perception of a natural harmony that included humanity might now help Americans become more attuned to nature within urban and suburban settings.

On my initial visit to Japan in May of 1987, when I finally laid the books down and boarded a plane for Tokyo's Narita Airport, a visit to Bashō's Matsushima Bay was one of the first items on my itinerary. I took the Shinkansen, or Bullet Train, north from Tokyo to the coastal city of Sendai, then transferred to the local that carried commuters and tourists out to the bay itself. Since the poet wrote, Matsushima has been celebrated as one of Japan's three most beautiful landscapes. My route from the station to the harbor was marked by plastic statues of the poet, posted along the sidewalk and featuring the large, bulbous nose that is his trademark. But wherever I stood to look across the water—from the ridge of an island attached to the mainland by a long foot-bridge, from the teahouse constructed on shore by the *daimyo* Date Masamune, from the Zuigenji Temple on the high ground farther inland—the view was dominated by the enormous smokestacks of a power plant. Not only were they far taller than any other natural or human form along the coast, but the tops were encircled by commanding red and white stripes. As the tour boats, their prows shaped like the heads of peacocks and dragons, cruised out through the islands, it seemed that they were bearing straight for these overwhelming verticals.

Even with all the careless "development" that is a fact of life in America, it seemed shocking that the Japanese would allow such a monolithic eyesore to be constructed at the focal point of one of their most revered natural and cultural sites. In the following weeks, however, as I traveled around the country with my Japan Rail Pass, I saw major construction projects just about everywhere I went. Even when taking a ferry to Hiroshima through the Inland Sea, I was rarely out of sight of a derrick on the shore, or out of sound of earth-moving machinery. The nineteenth-century prints celebrating this coastal landscape hovered in my mind; I looked through them, as through faded transparencies, at the gray emerging face of the new Japan.

Arriving in Hiroshima, I was taken out to dinner by several friends of a Japanese colleague of mine. We sat on tatami mats around a long, low table in the restaurant's upper dining room, relay after relay of Kirin beer loosening our tongues. One man, a professor at Hiroshima University, shared my interests in Japanese and American literature. As the conversation with him bobbed and turned, there came a moment when I could ask the question that had been growing in my mind. Could the love of nature so distinctive and central to Japanese culture survive the current boom of building, industrialization, and natural exploitation ?

With no hesitation, Professor Aihara answered yes. Take a stroll down any alley in Hiroshima, he advised me. Beside the doorways and in the windows I would see lovingly tended bonsai trees, set out to take the morning air. Or for that matter, he said, look down at the platters on our table. Tiny raw octopus were bedded on seaweed, looking just as they had when they were netted that morning. Chrysanthemum heads were arrayed around whole prawns and lightly grilled whole fish. Such meals celebrated the forms of nature; they were daily experiences of communion. Professor Aihara went on to remind me that practically every Japanese name derives from natural objects, that the graceful strokes of traditional calligraphy, too, grow out of the twining lines of grass, the drooping curves of willows. Nature was not just the background of Japan's culture: it was its heart.

I knew that these examples were true to the Japanese tradition. Bashō's poems offer *moments* in nature, not landscapes in the conventional Western sense. In my favorite of his haiku, a single raven on a bare branch hones the edge between seasons—*aki no kure* ("the fall of autumn"). The Ryōanji garden of Kyoto is another distillation of this microcosmic genius. A rectangle of fine, light gravel is surrounded by walls on three sides and enclosed by an airy meditation hall on the fourth. Fifteen rocks of varying size and shape are scattered down the length of the rectangle, a number of them rising out of thick clumps of moss. Though mature trees tower above the walls, the rocks and gravel, in their mysterious balance, become the onlooker's whole world. Some people have discovered in this arrangement a mother tiger leading her cubs across a stony riverbed. Others have seen an ocean in the ripples of raked gravel, with islands, or continents, rising up from the mossy surf. If one sits long enough on the hall's long wooden steps, though, this dry garden gradually conveys the more resistant, more refreshing integrity of *wildness*. Thoreau writes in *Walden* : "Nature puts no question and answers none which

we mortals ask. She has long ago taken her resolution."
Since the fifteenth century, this ten-by-twenty-four-meter
plot has offered to monks and visitors alike the unrespon-
sive resolution of nature herself.

The architect Ashihara Yoshinobu has pointed out in
his book *The Aesthetic Townscape* (1983) that the Ryōanji
garden, while separated from the surrounding landscape
by its walls, is not meant to be viewed by a person standing
inside it. Its balance and significance are available only
when one is sitting within the temple building looking out
at it. This follows from the special status of the floor as a
"sanctified" space in a Japanese building. Ashihara writes:
"It is from this elevated position inside that the landscape
outside is intended to be viewed." Two details of Japanese
culture confirm his distinction. One is the verb that describes entering a house, a tea cottage, a temple: *hairu*, or "to
go up." The other is the fact that one always leaves one's
shoes at the door, and with them leaves the dusty mundane
world.

I recognize another version of Ryōanji's ironic separation and enclosure within the walls of my experience. In
Go, the corners of the board offer the areas which are easi-
est to control; thus, the opening of a game frequently becomes a contest to see who can dominate in them. But a
strong player will sometimes prefer to place stones outside
the corners. Giving up secure territory for the sake of what

is called "outside influence," such a player begins in effect to wall in the center of the board. I have always loved this reference to the *inner* part of the board as the *outside*. Like looking at a Klein bottle or a Möbius strip, it bends my mind around. This paradoxical language also feels natural, though. Moving inward from the edge leaves a certain security behind. Aesthetically and psychologically, it is a venture out, into a landscape of potential.

But I'm still not sure Professor Aihara's "yes" was right. I spent a morning at Ryōanji, sitting on the long wooden veranda beside the garden. Every half-hour or so, a bus would pull up and a school group would bustle around the temple grounds. Again and again, a boisterous knot of blue-uniformed teenagers would walk out onto the platform and begin to count the rocks loudly. It's hard to take in all of the garden from any one vantage point, and the kids would usually stop with a laugh when they got to eleven and race off to the next building in the compound. The students seemed to be having a great time and were certainly neither noisier than American youngsters on a similar outing nor less attentive to the morning's miracle than, say, the occupants of most tour buses pulling up along the south rim of the Grand Canyon. The point may simply be that, in Japan, as in America, Edward Abbey's "industrial tourism" exerts its deadening effect.

The pace of our contemporary culture—the speed of our transportation and our mass media alike—makes it harder to find the meditative openness for which Ryōanji was designed. It seems pretty clear, too, that these Japanese teenagers frequently would rather eat a *hambaaga* from the golden arches of *Makudonarudo* than the cool, fresh offerings of sea and garden. They are also less likely to spend as much time as their parents did learning to write in calligraphic style. Pocket computers will remind them of characters they would otherwise have to learn through practice with a brush. The Japanese tradition of sensitivity to nature is today beset, just as American culture is, by heedless consumerism.

Japanese responsiveness to nature will certainly live on. Regardless of the changing outward face of the island, people will remember to begin their letters with a reference to the season and will continue to notice when the plum tree comes into flower, when the cherry blooms. And when the cherry branches are white, they will still gather as families beneath them, raising glasses of sake to the return of spring. Though these traditions help to alleviate the dreariness of technological life, however, they are finally no antidote to the environmental damage suffered by either Japan or America. I traveled to Japan looking for an alternative to the split between nature and culture troubling America.

What I experienced was a society that, no matter how different the traditional way of life from ours, faces the same essential problems.

In his book, Ashihara compares the refreshing balance of the garden at Ryōanji to the garish advertising displays that dominate downtown buildings in Tokyo and Osaka. "How is it," he asks, "that Japanese, so attentive to the design of exquisitely beautiful interior spaces, end up with such unsightly building exteriors? The only explanations I can find are in the priority given interior over exterior space that arises from the attitude toward garden scenery viewed from within and the characteristics of the 'architecture oriented to the floor.'" Looking at his photographs of building exteriors in Tokyo's Shibuya quarter, I can see what he means. Arrows, flashing neon signs, and towers erected on top of the buildings just to hold more ads combine to shatter any sense of architectural integrity. But looking at them quickly, before I focus on the *kanji* within the advertisements, I see nothing foreign to the disorder of Times Square or Los Angeles.

This visual connection strengthens my growing impression that, while the Japanese genius for nature has been expressed microcosmically and our American contribution has been in the development of national parks and

wilderness areas, we both suffer from a tendency to celebrate the precious aspects of nature hermetically. Just as
Ryōanji is enclosed within a wall, so too our wilderness
areas are bounded by a congressional mandate, decreeing
that within them there shall be no permanent building,
lumbering, or motorized vehicles. The Wilderness Act of
1964 erected a high wall to protect and define a series of
precious landscapes. The negative implication of such a distinction, though, is that outside the wall nature can be
exploited without restraint, that cities are "beyond the
pale," outside the sheltering wall of wilderness. New York,
like Tokyo, shows the danger of such distinctions.

Perhaps our two very different experiences of space
have brought Japanese and Americans to the same predica-
ment. Japan has been a densely populated country for centuries, with a great deal of its terrain too mountainous to
support much settlement. The southern plain has thus been
dominated by an urban corridor since the seventeenth century, when it included the world's two largest cities. Small
wonder that the Japanese genius so early developed an
inward appreciation for nature, or that emblematic celebra-
tions of the seasons such as *bonsai* and *hanami*, or "flower-
viewing," should remain essential even as the Japanese
strive to sustain economic growth on their crowded islands.
America, well into the present century, felt empty to the set-
tlers from Europe. In the rush to have some visible impact

on the land, we achieved a record of natural despoliation distressing even to ourselves. By the outbreak of the Civil War, vast herds of buffalo had been slaughtered, and much of New England had been deforested. Our wilderness areas were a belated decision to draw the line, remanding a few last patches of unspoiled nature into protective custody.

I celebrate the genius of protective and enhancing enclosure that has brought us the gardens of Japan and the wilderness legislation of America. But their hermetic limitations become clearer as we confront the global nature of environmental devastation in our time. Neither the garden at Ryōanji nor Alaska's Gates of the Arctic can be separated from the larger degradation of life on earth. Natural integrity can never be exclusive. Following my visit to Matsushima, hundreds of square miles of Prince William Sound were covered with oil slick, as blackened seals, otters, fish, and birds washed ashore. The millions of acres of wilderness set aside in the interior of that state can never correct or compensate for such a disaster in the area traded off to industrial and commercial development. Nor can the *bonsai* of Hiroshima replace or make up for the disappearing rain forests of Brazil. Carefulness identifies the mountains with the sea, and sees the balance rooted in the woods of opposing hemispheres. The love of nature must be comprehensive.

The environmental disasters suffered by, and perpetrated by, Japan and America do not mean that our natural visions of nature were false, nor that the hermetic beauties of garden and wilderness were a mistake. They show instead that these insights must now be developed further. In a game of Go, the enclosing energies of black and white propel the game beyond boxes and into a swirl of interfolding patterns—a beautiful complexity of design beyond either player's intention or control. In his essay "The Land Ethic," from *A Sand County Almanac* (1949), Aldo Leopold describes human history as an extension of ethical relations to broader and broader circles of life, and finally to the land itself. For Leopold, such a mature ethical vision will grow out of "love, respect, and admiration for land, and a high regard for its value. By value, I of course mean something far broader than mere economic value; I mean value in the philosophical sense." Love for the land has been nurtured in the garden, heightened in the wilderness. Now, perhaps, we can find the ways to express and enact it more expansively, more consistently.

Literature, in conveying the Japanese tradition of sensitivity to nature, did not mislead me. Poets of nature are not policy-makers but prophets, telling us what we need to do if we are to remember where we are. In America, as in Japan, we have our prophets. Thoreau, one of the first writers to point America to the East, serves as a bridge between America and Japan today, in his statement: "In wildness is the preservation of the world." John Muir, as much as he admired Thoreau, objected that Concord was no place to experience nature. What could that region of towns and farms, puckerbrush and second-growth woods, have to do with wildness? When Muir came up with his own version of Thoreau's credo, he said, "In God's wilderness is the preservation of the world." For him, the sacred expression of wildness demanded the vastness and the dramatic contrasts provided by the western wilderness. What Thoreau, and the Japanese, may have understood, however, is that wildness is finally a quality of experience as much as an outward fact. A suburban creek, or the electrically dimmed sky above a city, can still be wild to one who brings to it openness of eye and spirit. A pattern of rocks and gravel can refresh and inspire city dwellers just as a passage through the high peaks can.

Wildness is thus an inward and essential state about which the wildness, like the garden, can remind us. In order to encourage such wild awareness, Thoreau urges that, wherever we may find ourselves, we "live in infinite expectation of the dawn." In much the same way, Bashō strengthens our natural identity with his simple, integral picture of life within the flowering world:

*Asagao ni*
*ware wa meshi kuu*
*otoko kana*

I am one
who eats his breakfast
gazing at the morning-glories.

(trans. R. H. BLYTH)

Recalling our own naturalist legacies, and learning about each other's, perhaps Japanese and Americans can learn how to value nature on both sides of the wall. No part of the earth is less precious, natural, or "wild" because it lies outside congressionally drawn and protected bounds. In the same way, the Ryōanji sea depends upon the beauty of the Inland Sea: they ratify one another. The placement of each stone in the gravel reflects the larger, nonhierarchical balance of nature.

We look at *bonsai* to remember the pine islands of a bay that has been cultivated by the wind. We hike into the wilderness not just to climb the mountains, but also to see grasses shining with dew. Looking outward, looking inward, we regain our bearings as human beings in community, sustained by and celebrating the physical earth.

## Topics for Discussion and Writing

1. Bashō's haiku about Matsushima serves, for Elder, as an example of language showing "a natural harmony that included humanity." How could such poetry help Americans (and modern Japanese readers) "become more attuned to nature within urban and suburban settings"?

2. Elder asks, "Could the love of nature so distinctive and central to Japanese culture survive the current boom of building, industrialization, and natural exploitation?" Discuss the various responses to this question that are mentioned in this essay. How do you feel about it? Is the "love of nature" an old-fashioned feeling, irrelevant to contemporary Japan?

3. "I traveled to Japan looking for an alternative to the split between nature and culture troubling America," writes Elder. "What I experienced was a society that, no matter how different the traditional way of life from ours, faces the same essential problems." Discuss the basic similarities ("the same essential problems") between Japan and the United States in the relationship between human culture and nonhuman nature.

4. Write an essay in which you develop your own "theory" about the relationships between nature and culture in Japan and America. Use examples from Japanese and American literature (including texts in this anthology) to support your discussion.

# Baring the Atom's Mother Heart
### (1993)

## Marilou Awiakta

ക

"What is the atom, Mother? Will it hurt us?"

I was nine years old. It was December 1945. Four months earlier, in the heat of an August morning  Hiro shima. Destruction. Death. Power beyond belief, released from something invisible. Without knowing its name, I'd already felt the atom's power in another form. Since 1943, my father had commuted eighteen miles from our apartment in Knoxville to the plant in Oak Ridge—the atomic frontier where the atom had been split, where it still was splitting. He left before dawn and came home long after dark. "What do you do, Daddy?"—"I can't tell you, Marilou. It's part of something for the war. I don't know what they're making out there or how my job fits into it."

"What's inside the maze?"

"Something important...and strange. I see long, heavy

trucks coming in. What they're bringing just seems to disappear. Somebody must know what happens to it, but nobody ever talks about it. One thing for sure—the government doesn't spend millions of dollars for nothing. It's something big. I can't imagine what."

I couldn't either. But I could feel its energy like a great hum.

Then, suddenly, it had an image: the mushroom cloud. It had a name: the atom. And our family was then living in Oak Ridge. My father had given me the facts. I also needed an interpreter.

*"What is the atom, Mother? Will it hurt us?"*

"It can be used to hurt everybody, Marilou. It killed thousands of people in Hiroshima and Nagasaki. But the atom itself...? It's invisible, the smallest bit of matter. And it's in everything. Your hand, my dress, the milk you're drinking—all of it is made with millions and millions of atoms and they're all moving. But what the atom means...? I don't think anyone knows yet. We have to have reverence for its nature and learn to live in harmony with it. Remember the burning man."

"I remember." When I was six years old, his screams had brought my mother and me running to our front porch. Mother was eight months pregnant. What we saw made her hold me tight against her side. Across the street, in the small parking lot of the dry cleaner's, a man in flames ran, waving his arms. Another man chased him, carrying a garden hose turned on full force, and shouting, "Stop, stop!" The burning man stumbled and sank to his knees, shrieking, clawing the air, trying to climb out of his pain. When water hit his arms, flesh fell off in fiery chunks. As the flames went out, his cries ceased. He collapsed slowly into a charred and steaming heap.

Silence. Burned flesh. Water trickling into the gutter....

The memory flowed between Mother and me, and she said, as she had said that day, "Never tempt nature, Marilou. It's the nature of fire to burn. And of cleaning fluid to flame near heat. The man had been warned over and over not to work with the fluid, then stoke the furnace. But he kept doing it. Nothing happened. He thought he was in control. Then one day a spark.... The atom is like the fire."

"So it *will* hurt us."

"That depends on us, Marilou."

I understood. Mother already had taught me that beyond surface differences, everything is in physical and spiritual connection—God, nature, humanity. All are one, a circle. It seemed natural for the atom to be part of this connection. At school, when I was introduced to Einstein's theory of relativity—that energy and matter are one—I accepted the concept easily.

Peacetime brought relaxation of some restrictions in Oak Ridge. I learned that my father was an accountant. The "long, heavy trucks" brought uranium ore to the graphite reactor, which was still guarded by a maze of fences. The reactor reduced the ore to a small amount of radioactive material. Safety required care and caution. Scientists called the reactor "The lady" and, in moments of high emotion, referred to her as "our beloved reactor."

"What does she look like, Daddy?"

"They tell me she has a seven-foot shield of concrete around a graphite core, where the atom is split." I asked the color of graphite. "Black," he said. And I imagined a great, black queen, standing behind her shield, holding the splitting atom in the shelter of her arms.

I also saw the immense nurturing potential of the atom. There was intensive research into fuels, fertilizers, mechanical and interpretative tools. Crops and animals were studied for the effects of radiation. Terminal cancer patients came from everywhere to the research hospital. I especially remember one newspaper picture of a man with incredibly thin hands reaching for the "atomic cocktail" (a container of radioactive isotopes). His face was lighted with hope.

At school we had disaster drills in case of nuclear attack (or in case someone got careless around the reactor). Scientists explained the effects of an explosion—from "death light" to fallout. They also emphasized the peaceful potential of the atom and the importance of personal commitment in using it. Essentially, their message was the same as my mother's. "If we treat the atom with reverence, all will be well."

But all is not well now with the atom. The arms race, the entry of Big Business into the nuclear industry, and accidents like Three Mile Island cause alarm. Along with me, women protest, organize anti-nuclear groups, speak out. But we must also take time to ponder woman's affinities with the atom and to consider that our responsibilities for its use are more profound than we may have imagined.

We should begin with the atom itself, which is approximately two trillion times smaller than the point of a pin. We will focus on the nature and movement of the atom, not on the intricacies of nuclear physics. To understand the atom, we must flow with its pattern, which is circular.

During the nineteenth and twentieth centuries, scientists theorized about the atom, isolated it, discovered the nucleus, with its neutrons, protons, electrons. The atom appeared to resemble a Chinese nesting ball—a particle within a particle. Scientists believed the descending order would lead to the ultimate particle—the final, tiny bead. Man would penetrate the secret of matter and dominate it. All life could then be controlled, like a machine.

Around the turn of the century, however, a few scientists began to observe the atom asserting its nature, which was more flexible and unpredictable than had been thought. To explain it required a new logic, and, in 1905,

Einstein published his theory of relativity. To describe the atom also required new use of language in science because our senses cannot experience the nuclear world except by analogy. The great Danish physicist, Niels Bohr, said, "When it comes to atoms, language can be used only as in poetry. The poet, too, is not nearly so concerned with describing facts as with creating images and mental connections."

As research progressed, the word *mystery* began to appear in scientific writing, along with theories that matter might not end in a particle after all. Perhaps the universe resembled a great thought more than a great machine. The linear path was bending...and in the mid-1970s the path ended in an infinitesimal circle: the quark. A particle so small that even with the help of huge machines, humans can see only its trace, as we see the vapor trail of an airplane in the stratosphere. A particle ten to one hundred million times smaller than the atom. Within the quark, scientists now perceive matter refining beyond space-time into a kind of mathematical operation, as nebulous and real as an unspoken thought. It is a mystery that no conceivable research is likely to dispel, the life force in process—nurturing, enabling, enduring, fierce.

I call it the atom's mother heart.

Nuclear energy is the nurturing energy of the universe. Except for stellar explosions, this energy works not by fission (splitting) but by fusion—attraction and melding. With the relational process, the atom creates and transforms life. Women are part of this life force. One of our natural and chosen purposes is to create and sustain life—biological, mental and spiritual.

Women nurture and enable. Our "process" is to perceive relationships among elements, draw their energies to the center and fuse them into a whole. Thought is our essence; it is intrinsic for us, not an aberration of our nature, as Western tradition often asserts.

Another commonality with the atom's mother heart is ferocity. When the atom is split—when her whole is disturbed—a chain reaction begins that will end in an explosion unless the reaction is contained, usually by a nuclear reactor. To be productive and safe, the atom must be restored to its harmonic, natural pattern. It has to be treated with respect. Similarly, to split woman from her thought, sexuality and spirit is unnatural. Explosions are inevitable unless wholeness is restored.

In theory, nature has been linked to woman for centuries—from the cosmic principle of the Great Mother-Goddess to the familiar metaphors of Mother Nature and Mother Earth. But to connect the life force with *living* woman is something only some ancient or so-called "primitive" cultures have been wise enough to do. The linear, Western, masculine mode of thought has been too intent on conquering nature to learn from her a basic truth: *To sepa-rate the gender that bears life from the power to sustain it is as destructive as to tempt nature herself.*

This obvious truth is ignored because to accept it would acknowledge woman's power, upset the concept of woman as sentimental—passive, all-giving, all-suffering—and disturb public and private patterns. But the atom's mother heart makes it impossible to ignore this truth any longer. She is the interpreter of new images and mental connections not only for humanity, but most particularly for women, who have profound responsibilities in solving the nuclear dilemma. We can do much to restore harmony. But time is running out....

Shortly after Hiroshima Albert Einstein said, "The unleashed power of the atom has changed everything save our modes of thought, and thus we drift toward unparalleled catastrophe." Now, deployment of nuclear missiles is increasing. A going phrase in Washington is, "When the war starts...." Many nuclear power plants are being built and operated with money, not safety, as the bottom line. In spite of repeated warnings from scientists and protests from the public, the linear-thinking people continue to ignore the nature of the atom. They act irreverently. They think they're in control. One day a spark....

I look beyond the spectres of the burning man and the mushroom cloud to a time two hundred years ago, when destruction was bearing down on the Cherokee nation. My foremothers took their places in the circles of power along with the men. Outnumbered and outgunned, the nation could not be saved. But the Cherokee and their culture survived—and women played a strong part in that survival.

Although the American culture is making only slow progress toward empowering women, there is much we can do to restore productive harmony with the atom. Protest and litigation are important in stopping nuclear abuse, but total polarization between pro- and anti-nuclear people is simplistic and dangerous. It is not true that all who believe in nuclear energy are bent on destruction. Neither is it true that all who oppose it are "kooks" or "against progress." Such linear, polar thinking generates so much anger on both sides that there is no consensual climate where reasonable solutions can be found. The center cannot hold. And the beast of catastrophe slouches toward us. We need a network of the committed to ward it off. Women at large can use our traditional intercessory skills to create this network through organizations, through education and through weaving together conscientious protagonists in industry, science and government. Women who are professionals in these fields should share equally in policy making.

Our energies may fuse with energies of others in ways we cannot foresee. I think of two groups of protesters who came to Diablo Canyon, California, in the fall of 1981. Women and men protested the activation of a nuclear power plant so near an earthquake fault. The first group numbered nearly three thousand. The protest was effective, but it says much about the dominant, holistic mode of American thought that an article about the second group was buried in the middle of a San Francisco newspaper.

After the three thousand had left Diablo Canyon to wind and silence, a band of about eighty Chumash Indians came to the site of the power plant. They raised a wood-sculptured totem and sat in a circle around it for a daylong prayer vigil. Jonathan Swift Turtle, a Mewok medicine man, said that the Indians did not oppose nuclear technology but objected to the plant's being built atop a sacred Chumash burial site as well as near an earthquake fault. He said he hoped the vigil would bring about "a moment of harmony between the pro- and anti-nuclear factions."

The Chumash understand that to split the atom from the sacred is a deadly fission that will ultimately destroy nature and humanity. I join this circle of belief with an emblem I created for my life and work—the sacred white deer of the Cherokee leaping in the heart of the atom. My ancestors believed that if a hunter took the life of a deer without asking its spirit for pardon, the immortal Little Deer would track the hunter to his home and cripple him. The reverent hunter evoked the white deer's blessing and guidance.

For me, Little Deer is a symbol of reverence. Of hope. Of belief that if we humans relent our anger and create a listening space, we may attain harmony with the atom in time. If we do not, our world will become a charred and steaming heap. Burned flesh. Silence....

There will be no sign of hope except deep in the invisible, where the atom's mother heart—slowly and patiently—bears new life.

## Topics for Discussion and Writing

1. The opening scenes of Awiakta's essay emphasize a child's naive and yet very real fear of atomic energy. What connections are there, if any, between this twentieth-century fear of and fascination with the atom and the attitudes of earlier human generations towards the natural world? Explain how this essay is a kind of nature writing like the other texts in this book.

2. What does Awiakta mean by the phrase "the atom's mother heart"? Discuss her explanation of this phrase. How does it shed light on the meaning of "the nuclear industry" in the world today? Why does the author suggest, at the end of the essay, that we must not "split the atom from the sacred"?

3. Awiakta quotes the physicist Albert Einstein as saying, after the 1945 dropping of the atomic bomb on Hiroshima, "The unleashed power of the atom has changed everything save our modes of thought, and thus we drift toward unparalleled catastrophe." Is this still a valid concern in the 1990s?

4. Just as Awiakta looks back into her own childhood memories and her roots in Native American (Cherokee) tradition to understand the meaning—the implications—of nuclear energy, the rest of us can try to understand this important natural and social phenomenon by examining our own experiences and cultural traditions. Write a paper in which you explore the singnificance of nuclear power and/or nuclear weapons in contemporary Japan. You don't have to take a stance for or against the nuclear industry—just *explore* this phenomenon from philosophical, scientific, and personal points of view.

# Environmental History Challenges the Myth of a Primordial Eden
(1994)

## Martin W. Lewis

ঌ

Although warnings of impending ecological crises focus our attention on the present and especially the future, it is becoming increasingly clear that many of our environmental problems have deep roots in historical relationships between people and the natural world. The field of environmental history, which has emerged over the last several decades, can help explain those relationships. It can allow us to see more clearly the many-sided intricacies of our environmental dilemmas and possibly help us to develop reforms.

But as environmental history matures, it is beginning to lead us into uncomfortable terrain, forcing us not only to rethink some of our basic structures of academic inquiry, but also to reconsider—if not relinquish altogether—some of our most cherished environmental myths. What we have learned calls into question the widespread notion that environmental trauma is reducible to Western industrial society's alienation from nature, as well as the idea that humankind once lived in easy harmony with the rest of the natural world. We must not, however, let discomfort or disillusionment lead to bitterness or apathy about solving environmental problems. Rather, we need more flexible scholarship and more realistic versions of environmentalism.

Environmental history is based on the two-part thesis that humankind has been massively transforming natural landscapes for thousands of years and that, in doing so, has continually transformed human society. The emphasis is on the complex interconnections between social and cultural phenomena and biophysical processes. Environmental historians thus have investigated such disparate topics as the ecological roots of the Industrial Revolution, the links between the development of bureaucratic power and of irrigation facilities in the American Southwest, and the role that the exploitation of natural resources played in the development of American urbanism.

Environmental history's prime challenge now is to outline and explain the long-term development of human pressures on ecosystems around the globe. This task necessitates incorporating a broader perspective, both temporal and spatial, than has heretofore been the norm in historical scholarship. Although environmental history is beginning to change, most work to date has focused on the United States and other Western countries and has limited itself to the last 100 years. A longer-term and more ecumenical approach would greatly strengthen the field.

A broader focus will require more active collaboration with colleagues in other disciplines. While historians traditionally have relied heavily on archives, a documentary record may not exist for many of the periods or societies that we need to study, and documents will never be able to fill in more than a modest portion of the total picture. If we hope ultimately to integrate the history of humanity and that of the natural environment, the archival history of the historian must merge with the prehistory of the archaeologist—and both must be joined with the geohistory of the paleontologist, the climatologist, and the sedimentologist. Finding ways to cross such disciplinary boundaries and, indeed, the barriers separating the humanities, the social sciences, and the sciences will present many intellectual challenges, but the benefits will be profound.

A longer-term historical view founded on multidisciplinary research already is forcing a reassessment of some of our most deeply ingrained environmental notions. No longer can we confidently highlight some relatively recent development—such as the scientific revolution, the Industrial Revolution, or the invention of synthetic organic chemicals—as marking the decisive rupture between humanity and nature. Environmental activists have tended to hold a vision of primordial innocence, to assume that, at some distant point in the past, people lived in harmony with nature. Now, that vision is vanishing, in some quarters being replaced with something that might be described as "environmental original sin."

For example, Paul S. Martin, a professor of geosciences at the University of Arizona, has argued unceasingly that some 10,000 years ago, late-Pleistocene Paleo-Indian migrants may well have exterminated some 80 per cent of all large mammal species in North and South America. Although Mr. Martin's thesis has been and will probably remain highly controversial, new evidence continues to bolster it.

We now know that mammoths and other members of the elephant family often survived longer on islands not easily accessible to human beings than they did in mainland areas, an occurrence not easily attributable to climatic or other natural fluctuations. Once people learned to cross the seas, extinctions followed in their wake. In fact, when one turns to islands and archipelagos such as Madagascar, Hawaii, and New Zealand, evidence that the early human occupants brought ecological devastation is now incontrovertible.

This new vision of long-standing human destructiveness puts environmental historians in an uncomfortable relationship with the broader environmental community or at least its more committed fringes. "Harmony" between people and nature—long the catchword of the movement—is being proved chimerical as historians and others begin to show that relations between humans and the environment in the past were often less than harmonious. Moreover, the very harmony of nature itself is beginning to lose its meaning. Ecological theory now emphasizes continual flux and random changes, rather than equilibrium. The vision of a perfectly balanced whole of nature, into which human beings ought to be able to fit themselves, appears increasingly tattered.

We find ourselves faced by a political and moral challenge that more than matches our intellectual one: how to construct a more sophisticated environmental vision, one taking account of the complexities of nature and of human interactions with natural ecosystems.

Widening our geographic scope beyond the United States—or the West—will similarly challenge some deeply held beliefs. The idea that European and North American civilization is the single, peculiar source of ecological destruction is at particular risk. While popular environmental writings picture humanity's decisive breach with nature as occurring at varying times, they almost always place it firmly within the confines of Occidental culture, from which it supposedly spread out to contaminate the rest of the world through the processes of imperialism and technological diffusion.

This thesis also is still found in many scholarly works. Yet it is without merit. Indeed, this notion rests on an inverted form of Eurocentrism—one that focuses on the West as the center of everything vile and destructive, rather than as the focal point of everything progressive and virtuous, as the old Eurocentrism did.

The myth of special Western guilt overlooks the destruction long wrought by human beings in other regions. Consider, for example, East Asia. In China, the extermination of wildlife species such as elephants, rhinoceros, and tigers—often organized and purposeful—dates back several thousand years and continues to this day, spreading far beyond China's boundaries. (Indigenous, low-tech East Asian pharmacology, advocating the use of natural nostrums made form such substances as rhinoceros horn and tiger penis, deserves far more censure than does the Western medical tradition.) Similarly, deforestation, soil erosion, and the transformation of diverse wetlands into monocultural paddy fields have long histories in East Asia.

In the maoist period, the Chinese state organized a virtual assault on nature, rooted in indigenous ideas (such as the notion that large wild animals are dangerous and must be driven away from human habitation), as much as in Marxian ideals of collectivizing agriculture. Today, south China is experiencing the most rapid burst of industrialization that the planet has ever seen, generating an economic boom but also massive environmental destruction.

I do not single out China as a special environmental villain, nor am I trying to absolve the West from responsibility for its very real environmental crimes. Rather I am arguing that from a broad environmental perspective, the East and the West are more alike than unlike. China's economic boom can by no stretch of the imagination be dismissed as merely the product of Westernization. We must realize that East Asia—and ultimately any other region of the world—may prove to be just as economically successful, and just as environmentally rapacious, as Europe and North America have been.

Disillusionment with some of our comforting myths hit me profoundly while I was conducting research during the late 1980's in the Cordillera of Northern Luzon in the Philippines, where I was examining the transition from subsistence agriculture to chemically intensive commercial gardening. I had expected to find a relatively harmonious way of life replaced by a market-oriented economy that had wrought massive ecological damage in the years following World War II. I did find abundant evidence of post-war devastation, but support for the initial postulate eluded me.

Pre-war agriculture, while perhaps less destructive than what took place after the war, also had produced devastation of wildlife, deforestation, and a fundamental re-engineering of the landscape. More distressing from my perspective at the time, however, was the fact that everyone in the village that I was studying wholeheartedly endorsed the transition to a market economy, despite being fully aware of the heightened ecological traumas caused by incessant applications of insecticides, herbicides, and fungicides.

I returned from the Philippines with my own myth of a primordial Eden shattered. Environmental history is now beginning to go through the same transition. The resulting disillusionment can easily result in malaise and cynicism, as environmental historians discover how deep the roots of the ecological crisis extend. Scholars must work to turn disillusionment to positive ends. Doing so, I believe, requires that we accept our urban industrial way of life, but that we struggle to reform it so that it will no longer consume the planet as we try to feed ourselves and supply our material needs. To create an environmentally sane and sustainable society, we must move into a high-technology future—one based, for example, on photovoltaic solar power and information-intensive industries. But we must not attempt to retreat to an Arcadian utopia that never existed in the first place.

## Topics for Discussion and Writing

1. What are the "environmental myths" that Lewis says we must now reject? Are these only American myths or are they common even in other countries, such as Japan? Does Lewis propose any new, alternative "myths" to guide society in the future? What will be the role of technology in the next century?

2. Is there, according to Lewis, such a thing as "harmony" between people and nature? Explain his attitude towards this concept.

3. Lewis attempts in this brief article "to construct a more sophisticated environmental vision, one taking account of the complexities of nature and of human interactions with natural ecosystems." Analyze and discuss this new environmental vision.

4. Lewis suggests that it can be very useful to experience "disillusionment with some of our comforting myths." Try to recall a time in your own life when you experienced such "disillusionment," an awakening from pleasant, but untrue, views of life. Write a paper about this experience. You might want to choose, as an example, a view of nature that once made sense to you, showing how you came to change your mind.

# Disturbing the Universe
### (1987)

## Betsy Hilbert

✐

Five thirty A.M.; the parking lot of Crandon Park is deserted. An empty plastic drinking cup crunches under the tires as we pull in. Nothing seems worth doing in the world this early. Ute and I climb groggily out of the car. Then the dawn blazes up out over the ocean, rose and gold across the sky. Everything has its compensations.

The beach is still in shadow under the brightening sky, and the dim figures of the morning cleanup crew make a clatter among the trash bins. The two of us are on a cleanup of a different kind this morning, amid the beachwrack and the crumpled potato-chip bags.

"Seen anything?" my partner calls to one of the crew further down the beach, who is slamming a trash can with particular vengeance.

"*No, Señora,*" a voice drifts back, in the soft, mixed- ethnic accents of Miami: "*No tortugas* today."

Actually, we don't want the turtles themselves; it is turtle eggs we're looking for, in their night-laid nests along this populous beach. Our job is to find and rescue the eggs of endangered loggerhead turtles, and to move them to a fenced area nearby maintained by the local Audubon Society, where the hatchlings can be safe from the picnickers and the beach-cleaning machines, and other dangers inherent on a public beach.

We begin our long walk south, where miles ahead the condominiums of Key Biscayne loom in the pale light. Pity the sea turtle who tries to climb their seawalls, or dig her nest in a carefully landscaped patch of St. Augustine grass. A series of grunts and swishes erupts behind us, as an early-morning beach jogger huffs past.

Ute's practiced strides take her up the beach almost faster than I can follow, distracted as I am by the pelican practicing hang-gliding in the morning air and the rippled sand in the tidal shallows. She stops suddenly, taking a soft breath, and I rush up to look. Leading upward from the high-water mark is a long, two-ridged scrape, balanced on either side by the zig-zag series of close, rounded alternating prints. Turtle crawl. Has she nested? Like all good predators, we sniff around a bit before deciding where to dig.

Just below the high dunes, in a circular patch about six

feet across, the sand has been conspicuously flailed around. She has tried to discourage nest-robbers not by camouflage or hiding, but by leaving too much notice; the disturbed area is so big, and digging in the packed sand so difficult, that the attempt would discourage hunters with less sense of mission than we have. We could poke a sharp stick into the sand until it came up sticky with egg white, as is the traditional technique throughout the Caribbean, but that would damage eggs we are trying to protect. Nothing to do but start digging.

Beneath the turbulence of the dry top sand, the rough, damp subsurface scrapes against the skin of our hands. We run our fingers across the hard sand, hoping to find a soft spot. When no depression becomes apparent—this time it isn't going to be easy—we hand-dig trenches at intervals across the area. Sometimes it takes an hour or more of digging before the nest is found; sometimes there are no eggs at all.

In my third trench, about four inches down, there is a lump that doesn't feel like rock or shell. A smooth white surface appears, and another next to it and slightly lower. The eggs look exactly like ping-pong balls, little white spheres, but the shell is soft and flexible. With infinite care, I lift the little balls out as Ute counts them, then place them in a plastic container, trying always to keep them in the same position they were laid. Turtle embryos bond to the shells, and turning the eggs as we rebury them might put the infants in the wrong position, with catastrophic results.

One hundred fourteen little worlds come out of their flask-shaped, smooth-sided nest. The eggs are spattered lightly with sand, and my probing fingers hit patches of sticky wetness among them, apparently some kind of lubricating fluid from the mother. The surprising softness of the shells makes sense to me as I dig deeper; hard shells might have cracked as the eggs dropped onto one another.

Carrying the egg container to the reburying place, I am glowing like the sunrise with self-satisfaction. Savior of sea turtles, that's me. Defender of the endangered. Momma turtle would be very pleased that her babies were receiving such good care.

Or would she? I look down at the eggs in their plastic box, and realize that she'd regard me as just another predator, if she regarded me at all. That turtle, if we ever met, would be much more concerned about my species' taste for turtle meat than about my professed interest in her offspring. What would I be to her except another kind of nuisance? Perhaps the Mother of Turtles might respond as the Pigeon in *Alice in Wonderland* does when Alice tries to explain that she's not a snake, but a little girl: "No, no! You're a serpent; and there's no use denying it. I suppose you'll be telling me next that you never tasted an egg!"

What was I to these eggs but just another nest- robber? Did I really know the impact of my actions, the extended chain of events I was setting in motion? With present scientific knowledge, no human alive could chart the course of that one loggerhead as she found her way across the seas. Where she bred and slept, where her food came from, are still mysteries. Not only are there too few scientists searching for the answers, too little money for research, but ultimately there are "answers" we can probably never have. Our ways of knowing are species-locked, our understandings limited by human perceptual processes. I was a shadow on a dusky beach, groping in the dark for more than turtle eggs, digging, shoulder-deep, in holes not of my making.

Suppose we save these eggs, and the turtles that hatch return years later as hoped, to nest on this beach? This land will never be wild any more; the skyscrapers that rise across Biscayne Bay bear megalithic testimony that the future of South Florida is written in concrete. The beach, if preserved, will continue public, and pressured, one of a small number of recreation areas for an ever-growing number of people. So there will never be a time when these animals can live out their lives without the intervention of people like Ute and me. Like so much else of nature now, the turtles of Crandon Park will be forever dependent on human action. Thanks to us, they are surviving; but thanks to us, they are also less than self-sufficient.

And why am I so convinced I'm actually doing good, anyway? Suppose more babies survive than can be supported by their environment, and next year there is a crash in their food supply, or that something we do, entirely unknowing, weakens the hatchlings so that their survival rate is actually lowered? Maybe we should just leave them alone. Maybe they would be better off taking their chances where their mothers first laid them, risking the raccoons and the beach parties.

None of us knows the final outcome of any action, the endless chain of ripples that we start with every movement. We walk in the world blindly, crashing into unidentified objects and tripping over rough edges. We human beings are too big for our spaces, too powerful for our understanding. What I do today will wash up somewhere far beyond my ability to know about it.

And yet, last year, five thousand new turtles were released from the Audubon compound, five thousand members of a threatened species, which would almost certainly not have been hatched otherwise. A friend who urged me to join the turtle project said that on a recent trip to Cape Sable in the Everglades he found at least fifteen nests on a short walk, every one of them dug up and destroyed by raccoons. Whatever chance these hundred fourteen embryos have, nestled inside their shells in the styrofoam cradle, is what we give them.

In *The Encantadas*, his description of what are now called the Galápagos Islands, Herman Melville depicted the sea tortoises of "dateless, indefinite endurance" which the crew of the whaling ship takes aboard. Melville pointed out that those who see only the bright undersides of the tortoises might swear the animal has no dark side, while those who have never turned the tortoise over would swear it is entirely "one total inky blot." "The tortoise is both black and bright," Melville cautioned. So, too, my morning beach walk has two sides, one purposeful, the other full of doubt.

Whatever my ambivalences may be, the eggs are still in my hands. Ute and I reach the hatchery enclosure and unlock the chain-link fence. We dig another hole as close in size and shape to the original as we can imitate, and then rebury our babies, brushing our doubts back into the hole with the sand. As we mark the location of the new nest with a circle of wire fencing, I am reminded that in the world today there is no way, any more, not to do something. Even if despite our best efforts there will never again be any loggerhead turtles, even if the numbers of the people concerned are few and our knowledge pitifully limited, even if we sometimes do unconscious harm in trying to do good, we no longer have the option of inaction. The universe is already disturbed, disturbed by more than my presence on an early-morning beach, with the sunlight glinting off the blue-tiled hotel swimming pools. While the choice is mine, I choose to walk.

## Topics for Discussion and Writing

1. Why are Hilbert and her friend Ute ("yute") digging up sea turtle eggs? How is this activity supposed to protect an endangered species?

2. "Did I really know the impact of my actions, the extended chain of events I was setting in motion?" asks Hilbert. Why is this an important question for environmental activists to ask? Should uncertainty about the ultimate effect of their actions stop people from trying to help? Discuss Hilbert's decision.

3. Does Hilbert's essay change the way you think about environmental activism? Does it make sense that activists can experience, at the same time, both doubt and a strong sense of purpose? Discuss some of the current environmental issues in Japan (damming rivers, destroying sensitive "wetlands," industrial and nuclear waste disposal, logging overseas and bringing wood back to Japan, and so forth), and consider some of the arguments for taking action or not taking action.

4. Choose one particular environmental issue pertinent to your home area in Japan and do some research on this topic: collect books and articles, call or meet with people who are actively involved with this issue, and if possible even attend meetings or visit places that will help you to understand the current situation. Then write a paper, like Hilbert's essay, that not only provides information, but shows your own efforts to decide whether to "walk" or not.

# The Clan of One-Breasted Women
### (1991)

## Terry Tempest Wiliams

๙

I belong to a Clan of One-Breasted Women. My mother, my grandmothers, and six aunts have all had mastectomies. Seven are dead. The two who survive have just completed rounds of chemotherapy and radiation.

I've had my own problems: two biopsies for breast cancer and a small tumor between my ribs diagnosed as a "borderline malignancy."

This is my family history.

Most statistics tell us breast cancer is genetic, hereditary, with rising percentages attached to fatty diets, childlessness, or becoming pregnant after thirty. What they don't say is living in Utah may be the greatest hazard of all.

We are a Mormon family with roots in Utah since 1847. The "word of wisdom" in my family aligned us with good foods—no coffee, no tea, tobacco, or alcohol. For the most part, our women were finished having their babies by the time they were thirty. And only one faced breast cancer prior to 1960. Traditionally, as a group of people, Mormons have a low rate of cancer.

Is our family a cultural anomaly? The truth is, we didn't think about it. Those who did, usually the men, simply said, "bad genes." The women's attitude was stoic. Cancer was part of life. On February 16, 1971, the eve of my mother's surgery, I accidently picked up the telephone and overheard her ask my grandmother what she could expect.

"Diane, it is one of the most spiritual experiences you will ever encounter."

I quietly put down the receiver.

Two days later, my father took my brothers and me to the hospital to visit her. She met us in the lobby in a wheelchair. No bandages were visible. I'll never forget her radiance, the way she held herself in a purple velvet robe, and how she gathered us around her.

"Children, I am fine. I want you to know I felt the arms of God around me."

We believed her. My father cried. Our mother, his wife, was thirty-eight years old.

A little over a year after Mother's death, Dad and I were having dinner together. He had just returned from St. George, where the Tempest Company was completing the gas lines that would service southern Utah. He spoke of his love for the country, the sandstoned landscape, bare-boned and beautiful. He had just finished hiking the Kolob trail in Zion National Park. We got caught up in reminiscing, recalling with fondness our walk up Angel's Landing on his fiftieth birthday and the years our family had vacationed there.

Over dessert, I shared a recurring dream of mine. I told my father that for years, as long as I could remember, I saw this flash of light in the night in the desert—that this image had so permeated my being that I could not venture south without seeing it again, on the horizon, illuminating buttes and mesas.

"You did see it," he said.

"Saw what?"

"The bomb. The cloud. We were driving home from Riverside, California. You were sitting on Diane's lap. She was pregnant. In fact, I remember the day, September 7, 1957. We had just gotten out of the Service. We were driving north, past Las Vegas. It was an hour or so before dawn, when this explosion went off. We not only heard it, but felt it. I thought the oil tanker in front of us had blown up. We pulled over and suddenly, rising from the desert floor, we saw it, clearly, this golden-stemmed cloud, the mushroom. The sky seemed to vibrate with an eerie pink glow. Within a few minutes, a light ash was raining on the car."

I stared at my father.

"I thought you knew that," he said. "It was a common occurrence in the fifties."

It was at this moment that I realized the deceit I had been living under. Children growing up in the American Southwest, drinking contaminated milk from contaminated cows, even from the contaminated breasts of their mothers, my mother—members, years later, of the Clan of One-Breasted Women.

It is a well-known story in the Desert West, "The Day We Bombed Utah," or more accurately, the years we bombed Utah: above ground atomic testing in Nevada took place from January 27, 1951 through July 11, 1962. Not only were the winds blowing north covering "low- use segments of the population" with fallout and leaving sheep dead in their tracks, but the climate was right. The United States of the 1950s was red, white, and blue. The Korean War was raging. McCarthyism was rampant. Ike was it, and the cold war was hot. If you were against nuclear testing, you were for a communist regime.

Much has been written about this "American nuclear tragedy." Public health was secondary to national security. The Atomic Energy Commissioner, Thomas Murray, said, "Gentlemen, we must not let anything interfere with this series of tests, nothing."

Again and again, the American public was told by its government, in spite of burns, blisters, and nausea, "It has been found that the tests may be conducted with adequate assurance of safety under conditions prevailing at the bombing reservations." Assuaging public fears was simply a matter of public relations. "Your best action," an Atomic Energy Commission booklet read, "is not to be worried about fallout." A news release typical of the times stated, "We find no basis for concluding that harm to any individual has resulted from radioactive fallout."

On August 30, 1979, during Jimmy Carter's presidency, a suit was filed, *Irene Allen v. The United States of America.* Mrs. Allen's case was the first on an alphabetical list of twenty-four test cases, representative of nearly twelve hundred plaintiffs seeking compensation from the United States government for cancers caused by nuclear testing in Nevada.

Irene Allen lived in Hurricane, Utah. She was the mother of five children and had been widowed twice. Her first husband, with their two oldest boys, had watched the tests from the roof of the local high school. He died of leukemia in 1956. Her second husband died of pancreatic cancer in 1978.

In a town meeting conducted by Utah Senator Orrin Hatch, shortly before the suit was filed, Mrs. Allen said, "I am not blaming the government, I want you to know that, Senator Hatch. But I thought if my testimony could help in any way so this wouldn't happen again to any of the generations coming up after us... I am happy to be here this day to bear testimony of this."

God-fearing people. This is just one story in an anthology of thousands.

On May 10, 1984, Judge Bruce S. Jenkins handed down his opinion. Ten of the plaintiffs were awarded damages. It was the first time a federal court had determined that nuclear tests had been the cause of cancers. For the remaining fourteen test cases, the proof of causation was not sufficient. In spite of the split decision, it was considered a landmark ruling. It was not to remain so for long.

In April 1987, the Tenth Circuit Court of Appeals overturned Judge Jenkins's ruling on the ground that the United States was protected from suit by the legal doctrine of sovereign immunity, a centuries-old idea from England in the days of absolute monarchs.

In January 1988, the Supreme Court refused to review the Appeals Court decision. To our court system it does not matter whether the United States government was irresponsible, whether it lied to its citizens, or even that citizens died from the fallout of nuclear testing. What matters is that our government is immune: "The King can do no wrong."

In Mormon culture, authority is respected, obedience is revered, and independent thinking is not. I was taught as a young girl not to "make waves" or "rock the boat."

"Just let it go," Mother would say. "You know how

you feel, that's what counts."

For many years, I have done just that—listened, observed, and quietly formed my own opinions, in a culture that rarely asks questions because it has all the answers. But one by one, I have watched the women in my family die common, heroic deaths. We sat in waiting rooms hoping for good news, but always receiving the bad. I cared for them, bathed their scarred bodies, and kept their secrets. I watched beautiful women become bald as Cytoxan, cisplatin, and Adriamycin were injected into their veins. I held their foreheads as they vomited green-black bile, and I shot them with morphine when the pain became inhuman. In the end, I witnessed their last peaceful breaths, becoming a midwife to the rebirth of their souls.

The price of obedience has become too high.

The fear and inability to question authority that ultimately killed rural communities in Utah during atmospheric testing of atomic weapons is the same fear I saw in my mother's body. Sheep. Dead sheep. The evidence is buried.

I cannot prove that my mother, Diane Dixon Tempest, or my grandmothers, Lettie Romney Dixon and Kathryn Blackett Tempest, along with my aunts developed cancer from nuclear fallout in Utah. But I can't prove they didn't.

My father's memory was correct. The September blast we drove through in 1957 was part of Operation Plumbbob, one of the most intensive series of bomb tests to be initiated.

The flash of light in the night in the desert, which I had always thought was a dream, developed into a family nightmare. It took fourteen years, from 1957 to 1971, for cancer to manifest in my mother—the same time, Howard L. Andrews, an authority in radioactive fallout at the National Institutes of Health, says radiation cancer requires to become evident. The more I learn about what it means to be a "downwinder," the more questions I drown in.

What I do know, however, is that as a Mormon woman of the fifth generation of Latter-day Saints, I must question everything, even if it means losing my faith, even if it means becoming a member of a border tribe among my own people. Tolerating blind obedience in the name of patriotism or religion ultimately takes our lives.

When the Atomic Energy Commission described the country north of the Nevada Test Site as "virtually uninhabited desert terrain," my family and the birds at Great Salt Lake were some of the "virtual uninhabitants."

One night, I dreamed women from all over the world circled a blazing fire in the desert. They spoke of change, how they hold the moon in their bellies and wax and wane with its phases. They mocked the presumption of even-tempered beings and made promises that they would never fear the witch inside themselves. The women danced wildly as sparks broke away from the flames and entered the night sky as stars.

And they sang a song given to them by Shoshone grandmothers:

| | |
|---|---|
| *Ah ne nah, nah* | Consider the rabbits |
| *nin nah nah—* | How gently they walk on the earth— |
| *ah ne nah, nah* | Consider the rabbits |
| *nin nah nah—* | How gently they walk on the earth— |
| *Nyaga mutzi* | We remember them |
| *oh ne nay—* | We can walk gently also— |
| *Nyaga mutzi* | We remember them |
| *oh ne nay—* | We can walk gently also— |

The women danced and drummed and sang for weeks, preparing themselves for what was to come. They would reclaim the desert for the sake of their children, for the sake of the land.

A few miles downwind from the fire circle, bombs were being tested. Rabbits felt the tremors. Their soft leather pads on paws and feet recognized the shaking sands, while the roots of mesquite and sage were smoldering. Rocks were hot from the inside out and dust devils hummed unnaturally. And each time there was another nuclear test, ravens watched the desert heave. Stretch marks appeared. The land was losing its muscle.

The women couldn't bear it any longer. They were mothers. They had suffered labor pains but always under the promise of birth. The red hot pains beneath the desert promised death only, as each bomb became a stillborn. A contract had been made and broken between human beings and the land. A new contract was being drawn by the women, who understood the fate of the earth as their own.

Under the cover of darkness, ten women slipped under a barbed-wire fence and entered the contaminated country. They were trespassing. They walked toward the town of Mercury, in moonlight, taking their cues from coyote, kit fox, antelope squirrel, and quail. They moved quietly and deliberately through the maze of Joshua trees. When a hint of daylight appeared they rested, drinking tea and sharing their rations of food. The women closed their eyes. The time had come to protest with the heart, that to deny one's genealogy with the earth was to commit treason against one's soul.

At dawn, the women draped themselves in mylar, wrapping long streamers of silver plastic around their arms to blow in the breeze. They wore clear masks, that became the faces of humanity. And when they arrived at the edge of Mercury, they carried all the butterflies of a summer day in their wombs. They paused to allow their courage to settle.

The town that forbids pregnant women and children to

enter because of radiation risks was asleep. The women moved through the streets as winged messengers, twirling around each other in slow motion, peeking inside homes and watching the easy sleep of men and women. They were astonished by such stillness and periodically would utter a shrill note or low cry just to verify life.

The residents finally awoke to these strange apparitions. Some simply stared. Others called authorities, and in time, the women were apprehended by wary soldiers dressed in desert fatigues. They were taken to a white, square building on the other edge of Mercury. When asked who they were and why they were there, the women replied, "We are mothers and we have come to reclaim the desert for our children."

The soldiers arrested them. As the ten women were blindfolded and handcuffed, they began singing:

> *You can't forbid us everything*
> *You can't forbid us to think—*
> *You can't forbid our tears to flow*
> *And you can't stop the songs that we sing.*

The women continued to sing louder and louder, until they heard the voices of their sisters moving across the mesa:

> *Ah ne nah,nah*

*nin nah nah—*
*Ah ne nah, nah*
*nin nah nah—*
*Nyaga mutzi*
*oh ne nay—*
*Nyaga mutzi*
*oh ne nay—*

"Call for reinforcements," one soldier said.

"We have," interrupted one woman, "we have—and you have no idea of our numbers."

I crossed the line at the Nevada Test Site and was arrested with nine other Utahns for trespassing on military lands. They are still conducting nuclear tests in the desert. Ours was an act of civil disobedience. But as I walked toward the town of Mercury, it was more than a gesture of peace. It was a gesture on behalf of the Clan of One-Breasted Women.

As one officer cinched the handcuffs around my wrists, another frisked my body. She found a pen and a pad of paper tucked inside my left boot.

"And these?" she asked sternly.

"Weapons," I replied.

Our eyes met. I smiled. She pulled the leg of my

trousers back over my boot.

"Step forward, please," she said as she took my arm.

We were booked under an afternoon sun and bused to Tonopah, Nevada. It was a two-hour ride. This was familiar country. The Joshua trees standing their ground had been named by my ancestors, who believed they looked like prophets pointing west to the Promised Land. These were the same trees that bloomed each spring, flowers appearing like white flames in the Mojave. And I recalled a full moon in May, when Mother and I had walked among them, flushing out mourning doves and owls.

The bus stopped short of town. We were released.

The officials thought it was a cruel joke to leave us stranded in the desert with no way to get home. What they didn't realize was that we were home, soul-centered and strong, women who recognized the sweet smell of sage as fuel for our spirits.

## Topics for Discussion and Writing

1. The title of this essay alludes to the mythological tribe of women known as "Amazons." Look up some information about the Amazons and then discuss the appropriateness of Williams's title. How does the essay itself indicate a progression from victimization to warrior-like defiance?

2. Why is it unusual for a Mormon woman, like Williams, to criticize authority? Do there seem to be any parallels between Williams's life as a Mormon woman living in Utah and the traditional place of women in Japanese society? Discuss any possible connections.

3. When a police officer searches Williams in the essay's final narrative, the author refers to her pen and paper as "weapons." Explain how these tools, and the finished essay ("The Clan of One-Breasted Women"), function as aggressive, political weapons. How is it that this kind of writing can change society?

4. Try to think of some aspect of contemporary Japanese society that you find disturbing, somehow problematic, and write a paper in which you describe this problem vividly and then either propose a solution or at least show how members of society can work together towards improvement. Use "The Clan of One-Breasted Women" as a model.

# About the Authors

**Edward Abbey** (1927-1989) was born on a farm in western Pennsylvania, but he became one of America's most famous nature writers because of his many books (both novels and collections of essays) about the American Southwest, the harsh and mysterious desert country of New Mexico, Utah, and Arizona. Abbey studied philosophy at the University of New Mexico, earning his B.A. and M.A. there; his M.A. thesis focused on the philosophy of anarchy, and the essay published in this anthology ("Freedom and Wilderness...") has its roots in this early work. He also spent a year as a Fulbright Scholar at the University of Edinburgh and went to Stanford University as a Wallace Stegner Fellow in creative writing. Abbey's *Desert Solitaire: A Season in the Wilderness* (1968) is considered by many scholars to be one of the most important works of recent American nature writing. His best known novel, *The Monkey Wrench Gang* (1975), led to the formation of the radical environmental group called "Earth First!"

**Marilou Awiakta** (1936-   ) is a Native American (Cherokee/Appalachian) writer who was raised in the shadow of Oak Ridge National Laboratory, Tennessee. Her books include *Abiding Appalachia: Where Mountain and Atom Meet* and *Rising Fawn and the Fire Mystery: A Story of Heritage, Family and Courage 1833*. Her writing alternates between harsh critiques of such governmental agencies as the Tennessee Valley Authority (TVA) and Oak Ridge National Laboratory which have dammed major rivers and helped to create modern nuclear weapons and mystical reveries about the connectedness of the human and the non-human. "Baring the Atom's Mother Heart," which first appeared in Awiakta's 1993 book *Selu: Seeking the Corn-Mother's Wisdom*, combines cautions about nuclear technology and wonderment about the mysteries of the atom.

**Wendell Berry** (1934-   ) was born in Henry County, Kentucky, a rural farming community in the American Midwest. He received his B.A. and M.A. at the University of Kentucky, and then received a prestigious Wallace Stegner Fellowship to study creative writing at Stanford University. After teaching for a year at Stanford and then for several years at New York University, Berry returned to his home state to teach at the University of Kentucky until his recent retirement. In addition to teaching, Berry has been a prolific poet, fiction writer, and essayist, and also a farmer. In books such as *The Long-Legged House* (1969), *A Continuous Harmony: Essays Cultural and Agricultural* (1971), and *Home Economics* (1987), he has studied what it means to be devoted to a particular landscape, to commit oneself to a sort of "marriage to the land." "A Country of Edges" comes from Berry's 1971 book *The Unforeseen Wilderness: An Essay on Kentucky's Red River Gorge*.

**Annie Dillard** (1945-   ) was born and raised in Pittsburgh, Pennsylvania. She has been writer-in-residence at Wesleyan University in Middletown, Connecticut, since 1979. Dillard became well known as a nature writer in 1974 when her book *Pilgrim at Tinker Creek* won the prestigious Pulitzer Prize for nonfiction. Her many other books include *Holy the Firm* (1977) and *The Writing Life* (1989). "Living Like Weasels" comes from her 1982 collection of essays, entitled *Teaching a Stone to Talk:*

*Expeditions and Encounters.* Dillard's acrobatic, metaphor-filled language changes ordinary daily experience into something strange, something extraordinary, awakening readers to the wonders of nature and the human mind.

**John Elder** (1947-    ), although born in Kentucky, grew up in Mill Valley, California, just north of San Francisco. Elder was an undergraduate at Pomona College near Los Angeles and received his Ph.D. in English from Yale University. For the past twenty years, he has lived in Vermont, where he is currently a professor of English and Environmental Studies at Middlebury College. Elder's first scholarly book was *Imagining the Earth: Poetry and the Vision of Nature* (1985). In 1989, he co-edited *The Norton Book of Nature Writing* with the prominent nature writer Robert Finch. More recently, Elder and Hertha Wong co-edited *Family of Earth and Sky: Indigenous Tales of Nature from around the World* (1994). He and his family spent 1990 in Kyoto, and the essay "Wildness and Walls" appeared in Elder's 1992 collection of essays about living in Japan; the book is called *Following the Brush: An American Encounter with Classical Japanese Culture.*

**Ray Gonzalez** (1952-    ) was born and raised in El Paso, Texas, on the Mexican border. He studied at the University of Texas at El Paso and Southwest Texas State University. A leading Mexican American ("Chicano") poet and editor, he has published two volumes of his own poetry and six anthologies of Hispanic literature. Much of his writing explores the meaning of dreams and memories based on his childhood in the rocky desert country of West Texas, a landscape of cactus, powerful heat, no water, and poisonous reptiles and insects. "The Third Eye of the Lizard" first appeared in Gonzalez's 1993 essay collection *Memory Fever: A Journey Beyond El Paso del Norte;* many of the pieces in this book explore how the desert shaped the identity of the writer.

**Betsy Hilbert** (1941-    ) was born in Brooklyn, New York, but has spent most of her life in Miami, Florida. She earned her B.A. and M.A. at the University of Miami, her Ph.D. at the Union Graduate School. Since the mid-1960s, Hilbert has taught at Miami-Dade Community College. She has specialized in scholarship on woman's nature writing and has worked for many years to include environmental studies in the literature curriculum at the college level. In addition to her scholarly work, Hilbert writes literary essays about the natural world, including the piece called "Disturbing the Universe," which first appeared in the Summer 1987 issue of *Orion Magazine.* This essay considers the meaning of her work as part of the Tropical Audubon Society's sea-turtle rescue operation in the 1980s.

**Linda Hogan** (1947-    ) was born in Denver, Colorado. A Native American poet, fiction writer, and essayist of Chickasaw descent, Hogan received her M.A. from the University of Colorado and has taught there since the late-1980s. She has published several volumes of poetry, including *Calling Myself Home* (1978) and *Seeing Through the Sun* (1985), and two collections of short stories. Her novel *Mean Spirit* appeared in 1990. In 1994, Hogan received a $50,000 Lannan Fellowship, one of the most important prizes for American writers. Her essay "Walking" first appeared in a special issue of the journal *Parabola: The Magazine of Myth and Tradition* devoted to the subject of "attention." The essay suggests the importance of paying deep, respectful attention to the natural world, going beyond the normal use of the physical senses.

**Martin W. Lewis** (1956- ) was an undergraduate at the University of California-Santa Cruz, and earned his M.A. and Ph.D. in geography from the University of California at Berkeley. He has taught at George Washington University and Duke University, and is currently an assistant professor of geography at the University of Wisconsin-Madison. Lewis's first book, *Green Delusions: An Environmentalist Critique of Radical Environmentalism*, appeared in 1992. Although he is not normally considered a "literary nature writer," his sharp critiques of the mainstream environmental movement are extremely provocative and well presented. The essay "Environmental History Challenges the Myth of a Primordial Eden," which was published in *The Chronicle of Higher Education* on May 4, 1994, argues that our best hope of achieving an "environmentally sane and sustainable society" will come from pursuing a "high-technology future," not from seeking a more primitive, non-technological lifestyle.

**Barry Lopez** (1945- ) was born in Port Chester, New York, but grew up in southern California. He was an undergraduate at Notre Dame University and attended graduate school at the University of Oregon. Although Lopez travels frequently to remote parts of the world such as the Arctic, China, Africa, Australia, the Galápogos Islands, and Antarctica, he always returns to his home in the woods near the McKenzie River, east of Eugene, Oregon, to do his writing. He is the author of many works of fiction and nonfiction. *Of Wolves and Men* (1978) received the John Burroughs Medal for outstanding natural history writing, and in 1986 he won the American Book Award for *Arctic Dreams: Imagination and Desire in a Northern Landscape*.

Lopez's powerful and challenging prose demonstrates a profoundly respectful attitude toward words, nature, and his readers. The essay "Apologia" was published in a 1992 anthology called *On Nature's Terms: Contemporary Voices*, edited by Thomas J. Lyon and Peter Stine.

**David Roberts** (1943-   ) is the author of several books on mountaineering and a frequent contributor to American magazines that emphasize outdoor adventures. Roberts was born in Denver, Colorado, and lived until the age of five in the town of Corona, where his father, an astronomer, operated the world's highest coronagraph. Although he began mountain climbing in high school, Roberts became a serious climber after joining the Harvard Mountaineering Club (HMC) during his undergraduate years at Harvard University, where he majored in mathematics. The essay "Five Days on Mount Huntington," first published in *Harvard Mountaineering* in 1967 and later collected in *Moments of Doubt and Other Mountaineering Essays of David Roberts* (1986), describes a trip he and three of his HMC friends took to a dangerous and spectacularly beautiful mountain in Alaska. In 1993, Roberts published another book called *Once More They Moved Like the Wind*.

**Terry Tempest Williams** (1955-    ), a Mormon woman writer from Salt Lake City, Utah, is one of the most prominent and impressive contemporary women nature writers. Williams has degrees in English and science education from the University of Utah, and she has produced several important works of nonfiction about her experiences in the desert Southwest, including *Pieces of White Shell: A Journey to Navajoland* (1984), *Coyote's Canyon* (1989), *Refuge: An Unnatural History of Family and Place*

(1991), and *An Unspoken Hunger: Stories from the Field* (1994). She was a 1993 recipient of the $50,000 Lannan Fellowship. "The Clan of One-Breasted Women" is the final chapter of her best-selling book *Refuge*, a powerful critique of the American government's secret nuclear weapons testing in the Nevada desert, west of Salt Lake City. Much of Williams's work suggests a special connection between women and nonhuman nature.

# Permissions